Aldus PageMaker®
A Visual Guide for the Mac

*A step-by-step approach
to learning page layout software*

Linnea Dayton and Janet Ashford

Addison-Wesley Publishing Company

Reading, Massachusetts • Menlo Park, California • New York
Don Mills, Ontario • Wokingham, England • Amsterdam
Bonn • Sydney • Singapore • Tokyo • Madrid • San Juan
Paris • Seoul • Milan • Mexico City • Taipei

Many of the designations used by manufacturers and sellers to distinguish their products are claimed as trademarks. Where those designations appear in this book, and Addison-Wesley was aware of a trademark claim, the designations have been printed with initial capital letters or in all capital letters.

The authors and publishers have taken care in preparation of this book, but make no expressed or implied warranty of any kind and assume no responsibility for errors or omissions. No liability is assumed for incidental or consequential damages in connection with or arising out of the use of the information or programs contained herein.

Library of Congress Cataloging-in-Publication Data has been applied for.

ISBN 0-201-40724-8

Cover design by Janet Ashford
Book design by Janet Ashford and Linnea Dayton
Set in Garamond Light Condensed and Franklin Gothic Condensed
by Linnea Dayton and Janet Ashford
Imagesetting by Laser Express of San Diego, California

Manufactured in Hong Kong
First printing, 1994

Dedication

To Paul, Gage, and Anaika
L.D.

To Rufus, Florrie, and Molly
J.A.

Acknowledgments

We would like to thank all the artists and designers whose work appears in this book. They generously shared their time and computer files and it was a pleasure to work with them. Special thanks go to John Odam for his many contributions and his expert refinements to our book design.

We would also like to thank our imagesetting service bureau, Laser Express in San Diego, California, for their dedication to the job of producing film from our electronic files. In electronic publishing endeavors, it's so important to have the support of output professionals who understand your goals and will work with you to achieve them.

Both of us are fortunate to be able to work at home, and so this book came together amid the support and welcome distractions provided by our families and friends.

In addition to being professional colleagues and co-authors, we are also friends and neighbors, so we would like to thank each other for many walks and many talks on the topics covered in this book, as well as on the weather, the arts, and our lives in general. It is a treasure to be able to work with a friend.

Linnea Dayton and Janet Ashford

Contents

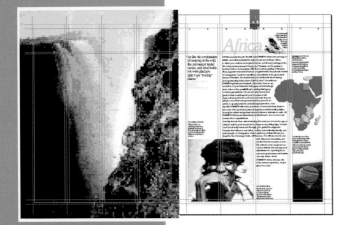

How to Use this Book   **1**

1   PageMaker Basics 2

Designing Layouts

2   Designing a Table of Contents: 1 8

3   Designing a Table of Contents: 2 9

4   Designing a Table of Contents: 3 10

5   Designing with Grids 11

6   Using Complex Grids 14

7   Making the Grid Visible 16

8   Designing a Brochure 18

9   Laying Out a Book Cover 22

10   Creating an Identity Package 24

11   Creating Professional Stationery 27

12   Designing Mail-Order Products 30

13   Designing a Mail-Order Brochure 32

14   Designing a Continuing Series 34

15   Designing a Magazine 40

Working with Type

16   Creating Initial Caps 44

17   Using Initial Caps: 1 49

18   Using Initial Caps: 2 50

19   Creating Custom Column Shapes 51

20   Varying Styles for Nameplates and Titles 54

21   Creating a Nameplate: 1 58

22   Creating a Nameplate: 2 59

23   Creating a Nameplate: 3 60

24   Using Vertical Headlines 61

25   Creating Department Heads: 1 62

26   Creating Department Heads: 2 63

27   Creating Department Heads: 3 64

28   Making a Type Specimen Book 66

29   Spacing Type 70

30   Setting a Mood with Type 74

31   Setting Fractions 77

32   Creating a Book Title Treatment 80

33   Typesetting Simple Tables 82

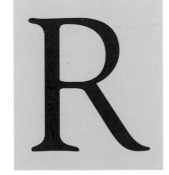

Working with graphics

34 Combining Colors 84

35 Illustrating with PageMaker's Drawing Tools 88

36 Using Type as Ornament 91

37 Framing a Photo: 1 94

38 Framing a Photo: 2 95

39 Layering Photos: 1 96

40 Layering Photos: 2 98

41 Layering Front and Back Elements 99

42 Making a Duotone 100

43 Creating Custom Screens 102

44 Customizing Photos with Image Control 104

45 Livening Up an Annual Report 106

46 Rotating, Reflecting, and Skewing Graphics and Type 110

47 Evolving an Electronic Approach 113

Managing production

48 Ganging Small Documents 116

49 Trapping 118

50 Producing a Book: 1 125

51 Producing a Book: 2 128

Contributing Artists 134

Definitions 134

Resources 135

Index 136

About the Authors 138

How To Use This Book

Knowing how information is presented in this book will help you find what you need to know. Here are some tips for using the book efficiently.

- Designing layouts
- Working with type
- Working with graphics
- Managing production

Covering the subject

This book shows, step-by-step, how to use Aldus PageMaker on a Macintosh computer. Chapter 1 briefly reviews program basics, covering the page layout topics shown here. It also includes keyboard shortcuts and tips for using the software easily and efficiently.

Presenting specific techniques

The subsequent chapters are of 2 types. In some chapters we have put together demonstrations of techniques that we think will be useful to virtually all PageMaker users.

Describing real-world projects

Other chapters tell how designers have used PageMaker on the Mac to design and produce a wide variety of publications. The finished work is shown in the title block of the chapter, along with the designer's name.

Overlapping shapes
Dramatic illustrations can be created by overlapping simple shapes. The winding road was created by layering a green ellipse over a light brown ellipse.

Working with Type

16	Creating Initial Caps	44
17	Using Initial Caps: 1	49
18	Using Initial Caps: 2	50
19	Creating Custom Column Shapes	51
20	Varying Styles for Nameplates and Titles	54
21	Creating a Nameplate: 1	58
22	Creating a Nameplate: 2	59

F
fills
    color, 18
    pattern, 6
flipping, 60
folding, guides for, 28
folios, 36
font chart, making, 91
for position only (*see* FPO)
Force Justify, 31, 56, 71, 74, 75
FPO scans, 13

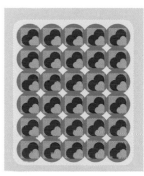

Creating a grid
We selected and grouped the row of 5 tiles, used Multiple Paste to produce a grid of 6 rows, and then added a solid background.

Showing and telling

In both the techniques chapters and the projects chapters, the how-to descriptions are highly illustrated, with brief captions that describe the illustrations. ⌘ *This symbol signals useful tips and shortcuts.*

Using the table of contents

The projects and techniques are grouped within sections of the book, according to the same topics covered in Chapter 1. To find a project by topic, check the table of contents.

Tracking down specific information

Many projects involve more than one technique and could have been placed in any of the several sections of the book listed above. The index in the back of the book will help you find references to a specific technique.

Browsing

Because the book is so highly visual, one way to locate a specific technique — or just to find inspiration or a jumping-off point for your own exploration — is to flip the pages of the book and look at the pictures. We hope you will enjoy the book and find it useful.

1

PageMaker Basics

John Odam

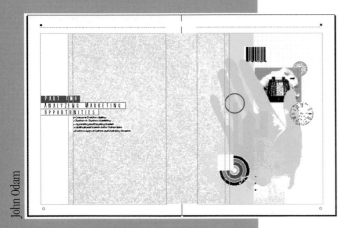

PageMaker 5 provides numerous functions for designing layouts, working with type, working with graphics, and managing production of printed publications. This chapter contains information about the program's basic functions, as well as tips for working quickly and efficiently.

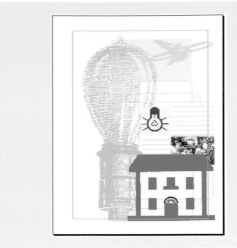

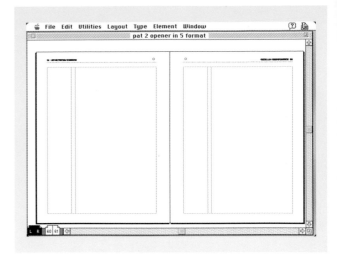

Designing layouts

John Odam, who designed the spread at the left as 1 of 7 part openers for a marketing textbook, describes the process he used to assemble it as akin to mixing sound in a music recording, with several tracks. He combined text; imported photos, scans, and encapsulated PostScript graphics; and filled shapes and patterned lines created in PageMaker.

Publication design begins in the Page Setup dialog box with the specification of page size and orientation, and whether pages are to be designed singly or in spreads. Layouts are often "anchored" with PageMaker's master pages, which can include column guides, guidelines dragged from the rulers, type, graphics, and folios (page numbers) that are used on all or most pages. Rulers and the Control palette help with sizing and locating elements precisely.

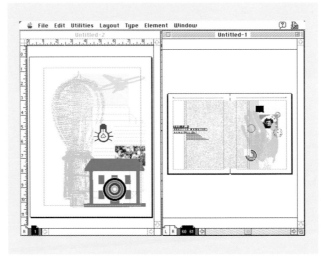

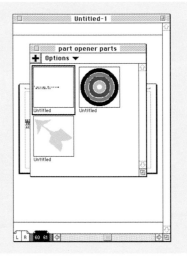

Text and graphics can be imported with the Place command. Or they can be copied from 1 open PageMaker file to another by dragging. PageMaker's Tile view (from the Windows menu) lets you see more than 1 file at a time. In fact, you can open and display on screen as many files as your computer's memory will allow.

You can also drag text and graphics from a Library palette. Open the Library palette by choosing Library palette from the Windows menu. Create a new Library by choosing New Library from the Options menu in the palette; open an existing Library by choosing Open Library. Since only 1 Library can be open at a time, opening a Library automatically closes the current Library. To add an object to a Library, select it and click the Add (+) button.

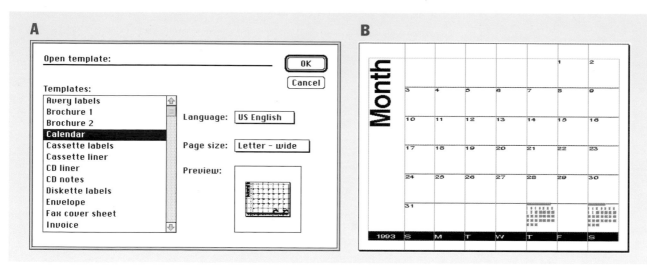

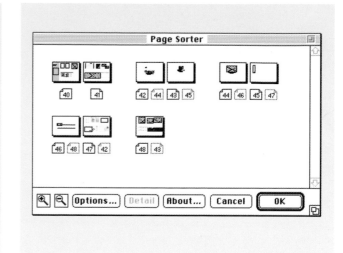

 PageMaker 5 comes with a set of predesigned templates for particular kinds of publications. To find the template you want and open it, choose Open Template from the Aldus Additions submenu of the Utilities menu (A). You can then modify the file to suit your needs, saving it as a Document and leaving the Template in its original form. Some of the templates, such as the Calendar (B), include instructions for use, set as text blocks on the Pasteboard of the template.

 Included with PageMaker 5 is an Aldus Addition called Sort Pages, which allows you to move pages from 1 location to another by rearranging thumbnails of the pages on screen. In its default mode, this Addition moves facing pages together. But single pages can be selected by pressing the Command key as you drag a page. Page number icons for moved pages show both the new number and the original number.

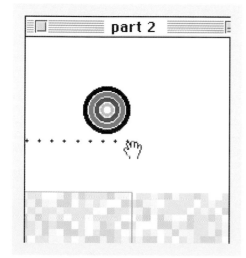

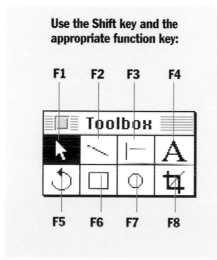

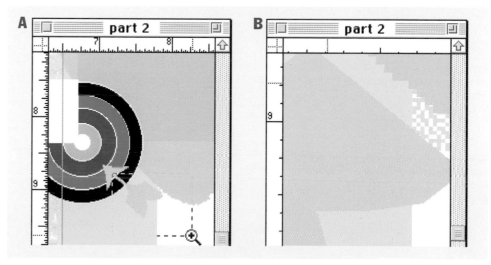

 You can get where you want to go in a hurry on a PageMaker page or spread by holding down the Option key to turn the active tool into the grabber hand so you can push the page around in the window with pinpoint, hands-on control.

 Each tool can be selected without dragging the cursor to the toolbox, by pressing the Shift key and a function key; use the keys indicated above. You can also use the keyboard to switch from any tool to the magnifier by pressing Command-spacebar. To switch to the reducer tool, use Command-Option-spacebar.

 In addition to the 8 views (Pasteboard to 400%) available in the View submenu of the Layout menu, or with keyboard Commands, you can also get up to 800% enlargement of a particular area by holding down the Command key and spacebar and dragging diagonally (A) to enlarge the area you want to view (B).

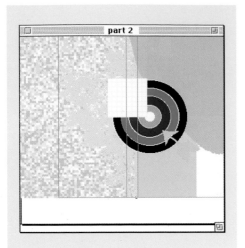

A

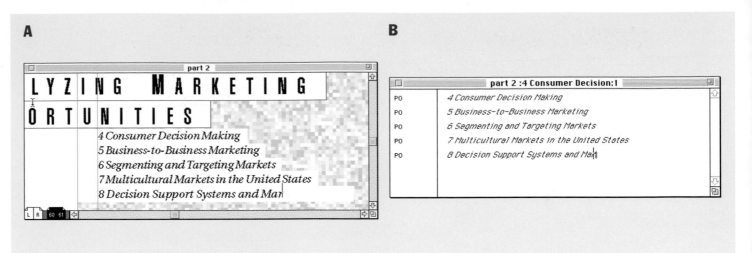

B

🍎 *In the early stages of designing a PageMaker layout, precise coordinates and measurements may not be important. To speed screen refresh as you move objects around in a layout, turn off the scroll bars and rulers (in the Guides And Rulers submenu of the Layout menu) and close the Control palette.*

Working with type

PageMaker comes with text *filters* (small programs that translate files from and to other programs) that allow you to import text files from word processing programs or from other PageMaker documents (through the Place command from the File menu) and export them (through the Export command from the File menu) to word processing programs. But you can also type text directly into a PageMaker file, either in layout view (A) or in the Story Editor (B). The Story Editor, opened by choosing Edit Story from the Edit menu, provides a full set of word processing functions — spelling check and search and replace, for example.

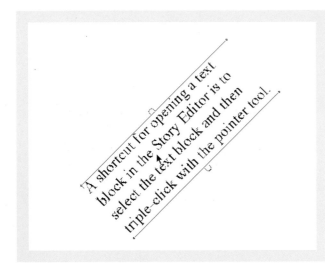

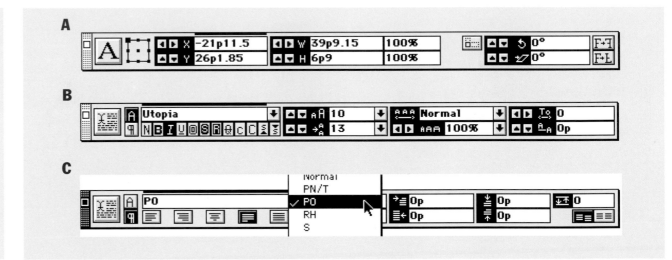

🍎 *In PageMaker 5, text blocks can be rotated to any angle, and rotated text can be edited. But sometimes it's hard to place the cursor and to edit at a slant. A shortcut for switching rotated (or any other) text blocks from layout view to the Story Editor, where text editing is quicker and easier, select the text block and then hold down the Option key and double-click.*

Once text has been imported or entered, it can be styled through the Type menu or the Styles palette. Control palettes for text provide a quick way to apply type specifications, either at the character level or at the paragraph level or to treat the text block as an object. When the pointer tool is active and a text block is selected, the Control palette provides placement, scaling, rotation, skewing, and flipping functions (A). When the text cursor is in a text block, clicking the "A" button puts the Control palette in character mode (B), with a font listing and controls for size, leading, character style and width, kerning, and baseline. Clicking the paragraph symbol button puts the palette in paragraph mode, with a Styles list and other paragraph settings (C).

🍎 *Even if you manipulate a text block or graphic by hand, the Control palettes can help by displaying precisely how things have changed.*

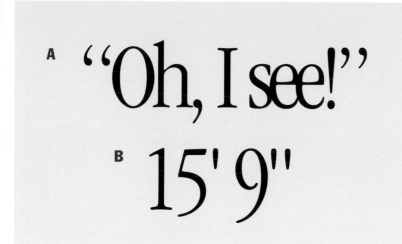

A "Oh, I see!"

B 15' 9"

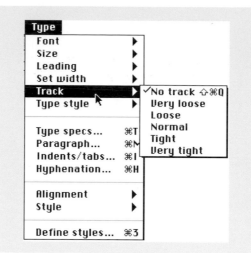

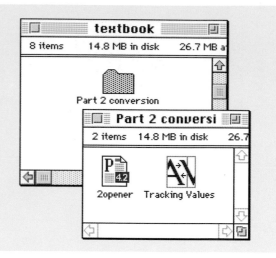

 PageMaker provides for automatic typographer's (or "curly") quotation marks (A) through the Place command (for imported text) and through the Preferences, Other command (for text typed in PageMaker). For text typed within PageMaker, you have to uncheck the typographer's quotes option temporarily to type inch and foot marks (B). For imported text, inch and foot marks that follow numbers are not converted.

 In PageMaker 5, Aldus improved the Track settings (for loosening or tightening the spacing in a paragraph or a selected range of text, without changing the width of the characters). However, when you open a document created in an earlier version of Page-Maker, the new Track specifications may change the "color" of the type (overall light or dark appearance of the text) and the line endings. To fix the tracking, Aldus recommends putting the document file in a folder with the Kern Tracks file from the earlier version, renaming the Kern Tracks file as Tracking Values, and then opening the document in version 5.

A

B

A

B

An inline graphic can be treated as text (kerning, tracking, and leading can be applied, for instance) 👋. And it can be treated as a graphic (with resizing, flipping, rotation, skewing, and cropping 👋.

Working with graphics

PageMaker can import many graphics file formats. The formats most commonly used in page layouts are TIFF (tagged image file format, used most for photos and other scanned images) (A) and EPS (encapsulated PostScript, for drawings) (B). If a file you want to import is bigger than 256K, PageMaker gives you the option of including it in the file, as it does for smaller graphics, or simply linking it, which does not increase the PageMaker file's size so much. Linked graphics are called by the print routine when a file is printed.

Through the Place command, graphics can be imported either as independent objects (A) or as inline graphics (B), which have properties of both graphics and text (they can be resized as graphics but given character styles as text, for instance). If the pointer tool is selected when the Place command is chosen, a graphic is imported as an object that can be moved around, resized, rotated, and so on, independently of any other object. If the text tool is active during the Place operation, the graphic is inserted at the cursor location in text and will maintain its attachment to that text.

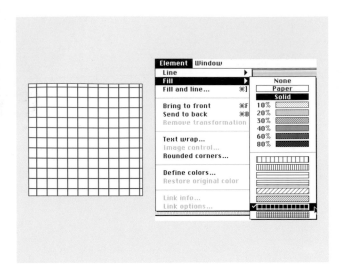

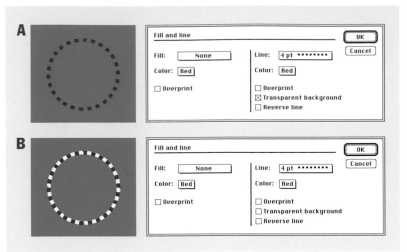

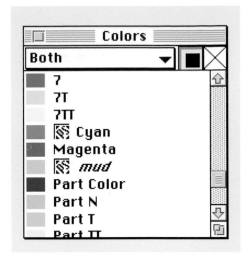

In PageMaker an object's line and fill can be specified separately from each other. Line and Fill colors can be assigned through the Element menu by choosing Fill, Line or Fill And Line, or through the Colors palette. Besides being filled with solid colors or tints, shapes can be filled with any of several patterns.

Choosing Transparent Background lets background colors show through a dotted or dashed line pattern (A). Otherwise the negative spaces in the line pattern are Paper colored — that is, they knock out of the background (B).

When EPS files are imported, their spot colors are imported into PageMaker's Colors palette, as are process colors from Aldus FreeHand. Imported colors can be applied to other objects in the PageMaker file. If you import an EPS graphic with a color name the same as a color in the PageMaker file, you can replace the color or not.

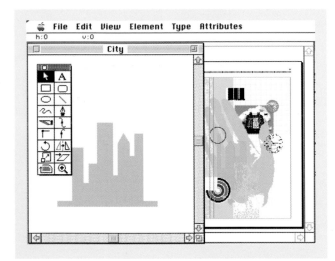

Photo courtesy of Digital Stock, Inc., Solana Beach, California

🍎 *With PageMaker 5 and Apple's System 7 or later you can update imported graphics without leaving the PageMaker page. Select the graphic, then hold down the Option key and double-click the graphic. This will launch the program that created the graphic so you can make changes. When you save the changed version, the graphic on the PageMaker page is automatically updated.*

🍎 *You can work at Normal display resolution for quicker screen redraw, and then zoom in on a part of the page to view a TIFF at High Resolution temporarily: Hold down the Control key and choose a View from the Page menu to redraw the screen. The next screen redraw returns to Normal graphics display.*

When you crop a TIFF in PageMaker, only the file data for the visible image area is sent to the printer, which speeds up printing. Also, resizing, skewing, rotating, and cropping are maintained for any graphic placed on a PageMaker page. That means that a low-resolution TIFF can be used for developing a layout and when a high-resolution version is substituted for printing, it will be positioned and manipulated in exactly the same way.

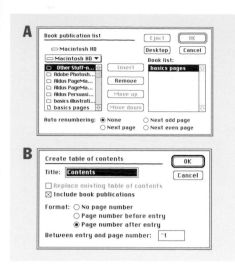

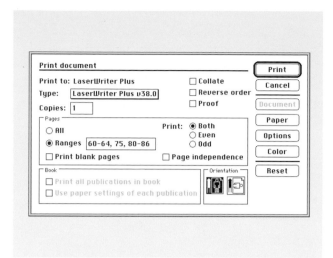

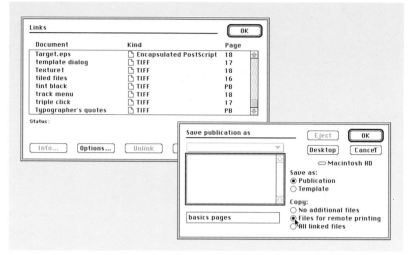

Managing production

PageMaker 5 allows you to customize document production and printing. For example, through the Book command from the File menu, you can gang publications (A) for purposes of printing, compiling a table of contents (B), or indexing.

You can specify discontinuous ranges of pages for printing. This means, for instance, that you can edit a document and then print only those pages that include changes. If you print more than 1 copy of a document, you can either print all copies of each page before you print the next, or you can Collate, printing all pages of 1 copy before printing the next copy. Reverse Order stacks the pages in front-to-back order as they come out of the printer.

When you send a document for output by an imagesetter, you can ensure that all the linked graphics are sent with the PageMaker file. First choose Links from the File menu to see a list of all the files linked to your document. Locate or check any files that have a "?" (indicating that the file cannot be found) or a triangle (the file has been updated since linking). After locating files and updating links, choose Save As and check Files Required For Remote Printing to save all the externally linked files in the same folder as the document.

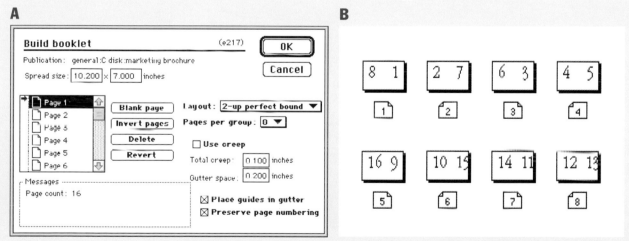

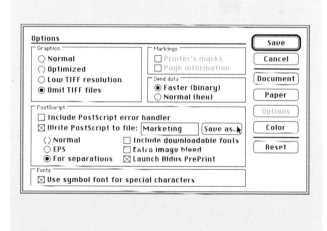

The Aldus Addition called Build Booklet lets you assemble the pages of a document with as many as 500 pages so that you can print several pages on 1 sheet of paper, then fold that sheet for binding. When you run Build Booklet on a file, a new file is created with the imposed pages. In the example shown here, a 16-page publication was imposed for 2-up perfect binding, so that 2 document pages, each 5 x 7 inches, could be printed on each imposed page, which would

be slightly larger than 10 x 7 inches, to allow for the gutter (the part that will be consumed by binding when the imposed pages are grouped into booklets, and the groups bound together along the spine). For our example, the output pages that would result from the settings in (A) are shown in (B). The page numbers from the original document are shown on the thumbnails; those for the imposed file are shown underneath.

In making color separations for printing, PageMaker 5 by itself can separate spot colors, or process (CMYK) colors defined in Photoshop. And it can separate EPS files that are saved in the DCS (desktop color separation) format and TIFF files if they were saved as CMYK TIFFs but not if they are saved as RGB TIFFs. To prepare a file for separation, the file is saved by choosing For Separations in the Print Options dialog box.

2

Designing a Table of Contents: 1

Sigi Torinus

A magazine table of contents provides information about articles and where to find them and also sets the visual tone for the publication, in styles ranging from sedate to experimental. This contents page for *Europa* magazine is built around the article titles.

Concerning "Noble Savages" and "Naked, Savage, and Cannibalistic People" – Depictions of Native Americans as Fiction

20   Frauke Geweke

The Meeting of the Two Worlds Has Not Yet Begun

28   Rigoberta Menchú

Ghosts and Witches of the Encounter

31   Edward D. Castillo

32   **Fantasmi e stregoni dell'incontro** - Italian version
34   **Les fantomes et les sorciers de la recontre des deux mondes** - French version
35   **Geister und Zauberer der Begegnung** - German version

1 Setting type

To design a contents page for *Europa,* a European cultural magazine, San Francisco designer Sigi Torinus set the article titles in 12/12.5-point Futura Extra Bold in 35% black, and set subtitles in the same font in 9/12.5. She set the page numbers and authors' names in Emigre's Matrix font at 12/12.5 points in black and indented the authors' names with a 0.5-inch tab setting.

To visually join each pair of title and author lines, Torinus used Paragraph Specifications from the Type menu to apply a Space Before of 14.4 points and a Space After of 4.6 points to the titles. This simple use of 2 typefaces created a table of contents that is elegant and easy to read.

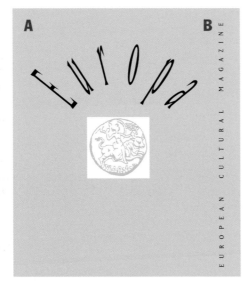

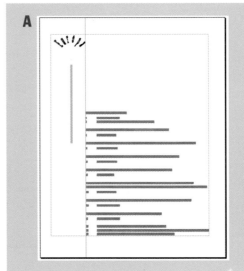

2 Importing type treatments

To create a logo for the contents page, Torinus used Aldus FreeHand to set the title in Matrix Tall on a curve over scanned art (A). She set a subtitle in Matrix Small Caps and rotated it to a vertical orientation (B).

3 Using white space

Torinus specified a 1-column page and positioned a guideline for aligning the left edge of the contents type with the right edge of the logo (A). Her generous use of white space lends a formal, open feeling to the finished

page (B). The magazine was printed in dark brown ink on a brown-toned recycled paper (see opening art).

3

Designing a Table of Contents: 2

Diane Fenster

The simple balanced structure of a contents page can be made more interesting with the addition of illustrations drawn from within the maga-zine. These provide graphic in-terest and direct the reader's attention to important topics.

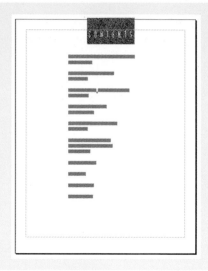

1 Creating a balanced layout
For *Intersci*, a magazine published by the San Francisco State University School of Science, designer Diane Fenster began by placing the contents list below a centered department head.

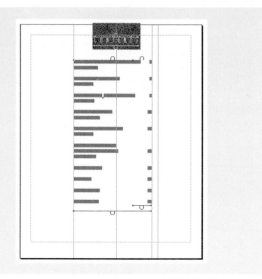

2 Using guides to create a grid
Fenster used guides to create a 4-column grid that is a little to the right of center because she wanted extra room on the left for illustrations. Page num-bers were set as a separate text block to allow for experimentation with their placement.

Toward a More Scientific Classification of Birds   1
Seth Mendelowitz

Biology – A Feminist Perspective   5
Rose Kirkham

Understanding the C_4 Dicarboxylic Pathway   8
Heather Henry

3 Specifying the type
The contents type was set flush left in 12-point Fenice bold and regular. The 19-point leading spread the lines and add a graceful amount of white space to the page.

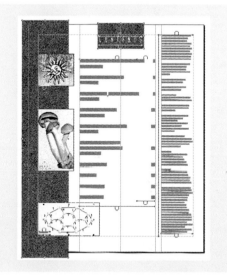

4 Adding a masthead, texture panel, and illustrations
Fenster positioned the masthead copy in a single column at the right, sepa-rated from the contents by a 0.5-point rule. An imported texture panel was placed to bleed off the left edge of the page. Illustrations were imported as TIFFs, resized and positioned, and set off with a hairline black box.

4

*Designing
a Table of
Contents: 3*

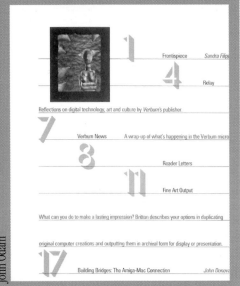

Oversized page numbers can serve as the design focus for a table of contents page or spread, as they often do for *Verbum*, a computer art journal.

John Odam

1 Using numbers to organize contents

Verbum's art director John Odam creates a new contents format for each issue. This one features numerals set in 72-point bold and regular Bookman followed by the title, the author, and a synopsis of the article.

2 Integrating the contents with the editor's letter

For the contents portion of this spread, Odam set the numerals in Bauer Bodoni with most of them colored gray and 4 colored black to call attention to the articles relevant to the issue's theme of "Blendo," or the blending of different art forms. Each numeral is followed by a heavy rule below in gray or black, and the article title, author, and synopsis.

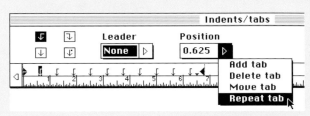

3 Creating a 2-page contents spread

Odam used Umbra, a font with a 3D look, to set 72-point numerals in 35% black for a 2-page contents spread, shown at left. In this case the article titles, authors, and synopses were set in 9-point Univers with 36-point leading and a 0.5-point rule below, and these elements and the numerals are run in together in the same text block. To lend order to the layout, Odam set tabs at regular intervals using the Repeat Tabs command under Position in the Indents/Tabs dialog box and used them to position the beginnings of titles and other elements so that they aligned with one another.

5

Designing with Grids

An underlying grid system of vertical columns and margins helps to organize pages, especially those that contain many elements.

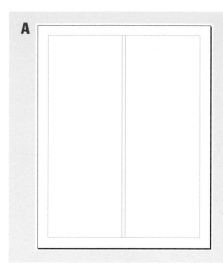

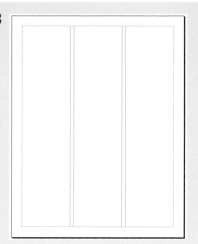

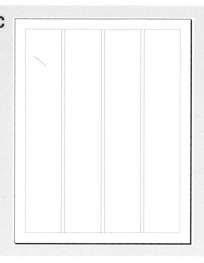

1 Setting up column guides

The easiest way to set up a grid structure is to specify column guides. We used the Column Guides command under the Layout menu to specify a 2-column (A), 3-column (B), and 4-column (C) examples. The Column Guides dialog box makes it possible to set the number of columns per page and the amount of space between columns (we used 1 pica or 0.167 inches). If the Column Guides are applied to the master pages, then these guides will appear on every page of the publication so long as Copy Master Guides is checked in the Layout menu. The column widths are automatically adjusted to be equal, given the specified width of the space between columns and the left and right margins specified in the Page Setup dialog box. We used a 0.5-inch margin all around for these examples.

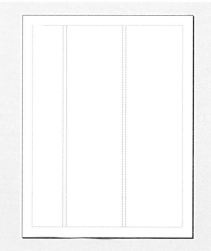

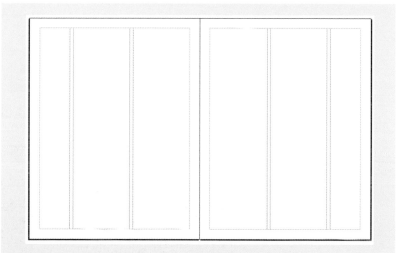

2 Creating custom column guides

Columns of unequal width can be created by specifying the number of columns you want and then dragging the column guides to the position you want. We created a 3-column grid with 2 wide columns for body text and a thinner column for captions and sidebars.

3 Setting up facing pages and master pages

Column guides can be applied to single pages or to 2-page spreads by checking or unchecking the Set Left And Right Pages Separately box in the Column Guides dialog box. To create a grid that is symmetrical across the gutter, with the thinner text columns on the outside of each page, we specified three columns, then dragged the column guides to the right positions, using the rulers as guides.

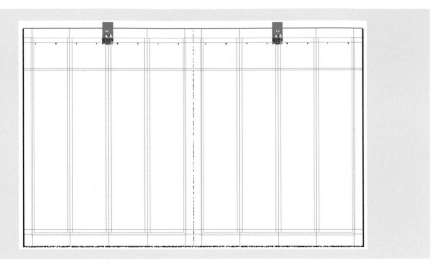

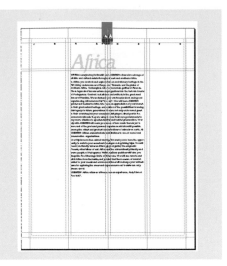

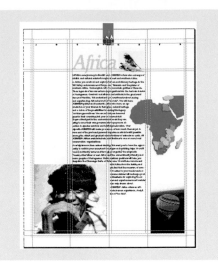

4 Designing a travel catalog

John Odam used a 4-column grid to organize the text and graphics for the Journeys company, which specializes in travel tours to exotic locations. He began by setting up a 2-page master pages spread containing a running head, a graphic icon, a textured border. The border was created by placing a TIFF scan of a texture and dragging it to cover both pages. Odam then drew two white filled rectangles and positioned one on each page to provide a white background for the text and graphics.

5 Adding body text and headline

After the general information pages, page 6 of the brochure begins the section on trips to Africa. Odam placed the introductory text within the center 2 columns and drew a tan box as a background. The title and body text are set in Korinna.

6 Adding graphics

Odam next added 4 graphics in the form of scanned TIFFs. These were used "for position only" and were later replaced with conventional photo separations to ensure the best quality. The 2 largest graphics were given a Text Wrap so that they repel the type around them.

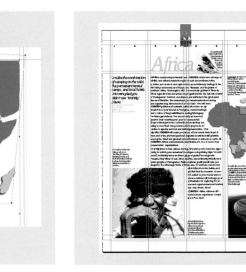

7 Adjusting text wrap

When a wrap option is specified for a graphic, Page-Maker creates a rectangular repulsion outline around it. For the map, Odam edited this outline so that it followed the curve of the graphic, clicking new points onto the outline and moving them to the desired location.

8 Adding captions and pull quotes

Odam completed the page design by adding captions in Helvetica Neue 55 in red and a pull quote in Korinna Kursiv Regular.

9 Aligning captions to the grid

The captions in the outer columns are left-aligned to the column guides, but the captions for the largest photo is aligned differently. Since the large photo is 2 columns wide, Odam dragged the right edge of its text wrap outline to align with the guideline that runs through the center of the center column guide. This determines the alignment of the type which is wrapped around the photo. The caption for this photo is aligned to the same center guideline so that it will align with the wrapped body text.

A

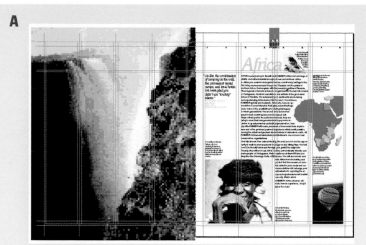

B

10 Finishing the page spread

Odam completed the page spread by placing a full bleed photograph on the left hand page. Once again, the TIFF is an FPO graphic, to be replaced later by conventionally separated film. The TIFF covers over the master page items (running head, border, and graphic icon) so that these will not show when the page is print. The page spread is shown here in screen view with the guides (A), and as it looks in the final printed piece (B).

11 Putting the grid to use

In the following spread, Odam used the grid to size his graphics to a half, 1, 2, and 3-column widths, while the text containing trip data is flowed into single columns. The grid helps accommodate the use of illustrations in a variety of size formats, both horizontal and vertical. The spread is shown here in final printed form and in screen view (inset).

12 Violating the grid

A grid can be used to arrange text and graphics in an orderly framework. But it can also be used to create drama by providing rules to break. For example, Odam gave extra emphasis to a photo of a tour participant feeding a banana to a monkey by silhouetting the photo, sizing it so that it overlaps a column guide, and wrapping the text around it.

6
Using Complex Grids

John Odam

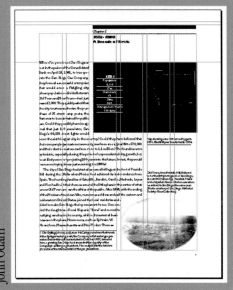

Creating an underlying grid system of 6, 8, or 12 columns provides a way to organize and scale graphics of many different proportions to fit with text on a page.

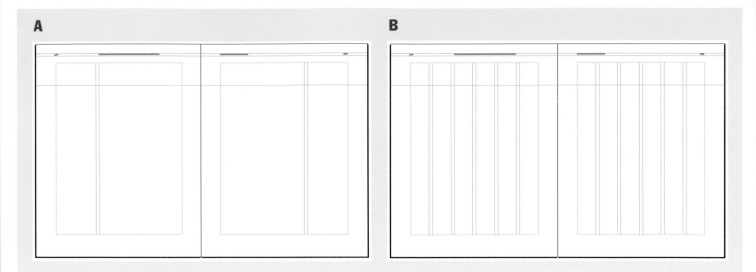

A   **B**

1 Using a multi-column structure

For a historical book on the San Diego Gas and Electric Company, designer John Odam wanted to use a simple page format with a wide inner column for body text and a narrow outer column for captions and sidebars. To accommodate just these elements, he might have set up a 2-column format on facing pages (A). But he also needed to integrate a large number of illustrations in varying size formats. So he set up the master pages to include a 6-column grid, intending to devote the 4 inner columns to body text and the 2 outer columns to captions and sidebars , and to use the smaller subdivisions as guides for sizing graphic elements (B).

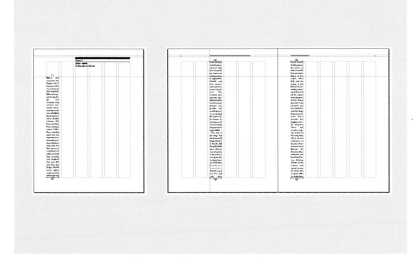

2 Placing the body text

Odam's first step was to import the body text from a word processor file. He did not use the Autoflow feature because it would have placed the text into each of the 6 columns on each page. Instead he held down the Shift key for semi-automatic text flow and clicked to place the text into the first column on each right-hand page and the third column on each left-hand page.

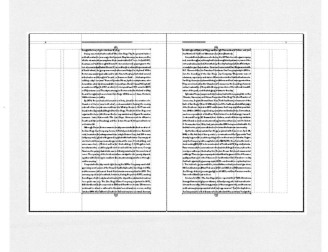

3 Spreading the text across 4 columns

Next Odam went back to page 1 and dragged the lower right handle of each text block to the right to reflow the text so that it spread across 4 columns. He repeated this process for each page.

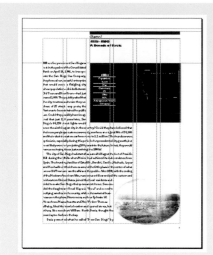

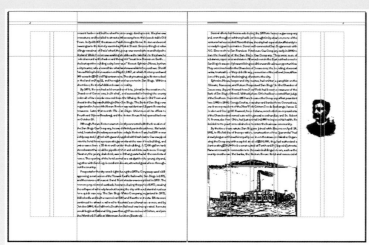

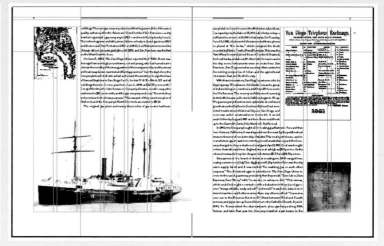

4 Adding illustrations

Odam scanned the illustrations and placed them on the appropriate pages, according to the content of the body text. Depending on the proportions of the graphic and the requirements of the text, Odam sized the imported graphics to a variety of widths, using the 6-column grid as a guide. He used his 266 dpi TIFF scans as final art.

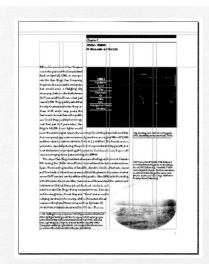

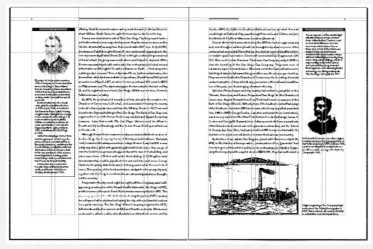

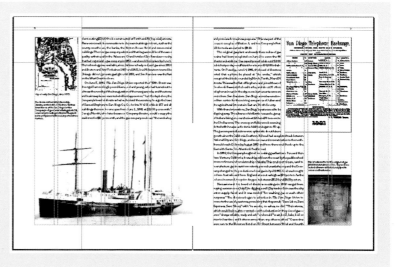

5 Adding sidebars and captions

Odam completed the page layout by adding captions and sidebars, using either 2 or 3 of the 6 columns. The captions and sidebar text were set in a sans serif face to contrast with the serif face used for the body text.

7

Making the Grid Visible

A design grid that is used to organize the elements of a page is usually a pattern of columns and margins that appear only as on-screen guides. But designers sometimes choose to make the grid visible as part of the page design, by drawing rules that print along with type and graphics.

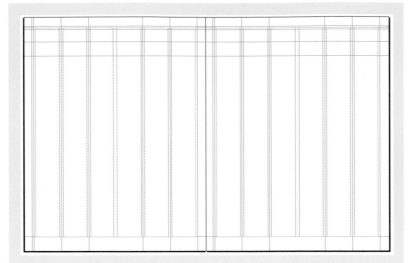

1 Creating master pages

For an annual report for the Steri-Oss company, San Diego designer Tom Gould set up a flexible grid system of 6 columns per page by opening the master pages and specifying 6 columns in the Column Guides dialog box, available from the Layout menu. He specified a Space Between Columns of 1 pica and added guidelines to help in the placement of rules and other elements.

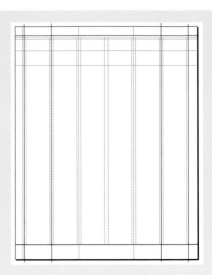

2 Drawing grid lines for a 1-column layout

Using the columns and guidelines, Gould drew 0.5-point black lines along the outside edges of the type area and through the 2 outermost spaces between the columns of the first right-hand page.

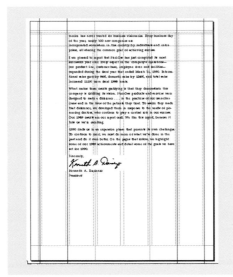

3 Adding a text block

Gould then entered the introductory text in a single block spread across the center 4 columns of the page. The text was set in 11/16-point Stone Serif, and a scanned signature was placed as an imported TIFF file.

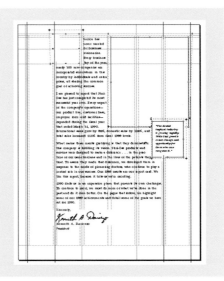

4 Preparing a keyline

Gould drew a black keyline box for a photograph and a box with no line as a placeholder for an initial capital he planned to have stripped in later. He drew a border for a pull quote and applied a Text Wrap to all three boxes.

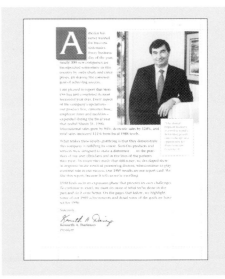

5 Printing the page

Text for the pull quote was set in 9/12-point Stone Serif bold italic. The finished page was printed with the body text, signature, and photo in black, the initial cap and pull quote in green, and the grid lines in metallic silver.

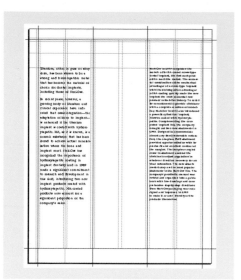
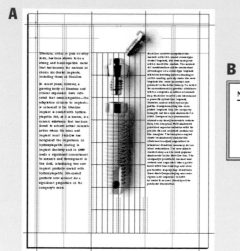
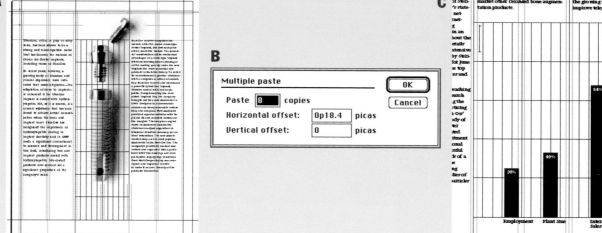

A

B

Multiple paste

Paste **8** copies

Horizontal offset: **0p18.4** picas

Vertical offset: **0** picas

OK

Cancel

C

6 Creating a 3-column layout

For page 2 Gould drew 0.5-point black grid lines that subdivide the page into a 3-column format. He set 1 column of body type in 11/16-point Stone Serif and a column of caption type in 9/12-point Stone Serif bold.

7 Creating grids with Multiple Paste

To convey his client's concern with precise measurement, Gould built on the grid theme by drawing a pattern of lines inside the center column of page 2 as a background for a photo of one of the company's dental implants (A). To make sure the 9 interior vertical lines were evenly spaced, Gould measured the width of the column, divided it by 10 to get 18.4 points, drew the first line, and positioned it 18.4 points to the right of the left-hand column border line. Then he copied the line and entered values in the Multiple Paste dialog box (under the Edit menu) to create 8 copies that were offset 18.4 points horizontally (B). He also used Multiple Paste to space the horizontal lines for the pattern and used it again to create grid lines for a chart (C).

8 Combining formats in 1 spread

Gould finished the page by adding a title bar and pull quote and then set up page 3 in the same single-column format he had used for page 1. The underlying grid system of 6 columns per page helps make the differing column formats of the 2-page spread work well together.

9 Adding PostScript graphics

The final spread of the report also features a 1-column page set off against a 3-column page. For the 3-column page Gould added a company logo created in Aldus FreeHand and a world map that incorporates the same kind of line pattern used on page 2. Gould created the entire map, including grid lines, in FreeHand and imported into PageMaker as an EPS file.

8

Designing a Brochure

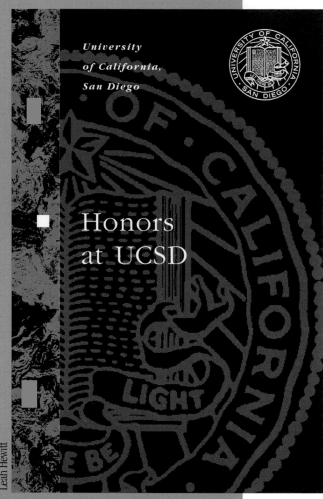

A striking cover and elegant inside pages for a university pamphlet were created using imported scanned elements.

Leah Hewitt

1 Setting up the page size

Designer Leah Hewitt of the Publications Department at the University of California at San Diego (UCSD) used PageMaker to create a cover and inside pages for a pamphlet about an honors program. She began by using the Page Setup command to specify a page size of 8.75 x 11 inches for a continuous front and back cover for the 5.5 x 8.75-inch pamphlet.

2 Specifying a Pantone background color

To create a purple background, Hewitt opened the Define Colors dialog box and chose PMS 269, which then appeared as a choice in the Colors palette. She drew a rectangle to cover the entire page plus a 0.125-inch bleed all around, and filled it with the purple by choosing Solid from the Fill submenu (under the Element menu), and clicking on PMS 269 in the Colors palette.

3 Scanning a university seal

The University's Publications Department had previously scanned a copy of the seal of the University of California. The scan was saved as a TIFF in Bitmap (black-and-white) mode so that its white parts would be transparent when it was imported into PageMaker. The seal image was about 2.25 inches in diameter.

4 Enlarging and placing the seal on the background

Hewitt placed the TIFF in PageMaker, enlarged it to fill most of the cover, then cropped the TIFF to the bottom of the page. To color the TIFF for the purpose of displaying it on-screen, Hewitt specified a process color to approximate the 80 percent tint of PMS 269 she planned to use. She clicked on this color in the Colors palette to apply it to the selected TIFF.

5 Scanning another university seal

The UCSD seal was scanned and saved as a bitmap TIFF so that it would be transparent when placed in PageMaker. The image was about 3 inches in diameter at 300 dpi.

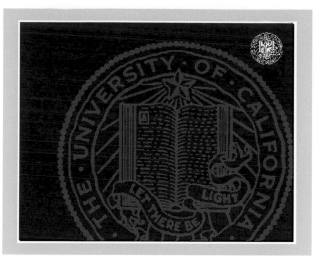

6 Reversing and placing the seal

Hewitt placed this seal in the pamphlet file, reduced it to about 1.25 inches wide, and specified a color of Paper, which was set to the default of white. Reducing the size of the UCSD seal effectively increased its resolution. The sharpness of the small seal provides a contrast with the irregularities and pixellated look of the enlarged seal.

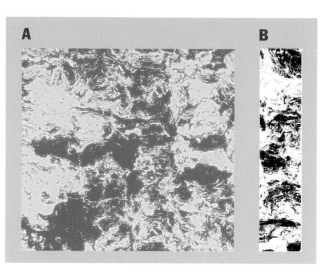

7 Scanning a bark paper texture

To create a texture for the spine of the pamphlet, Hewitt scanned a piece of rough bark paper (A), again saving it in bitmap mode so that it would be transparent when imported into PageMaker. She cropped the image to a vertical rectangle close to the size she needed (B).

8 Creating a two-color texture

To provide a contrasting background for the texture, Hewitt drew a vertical rectangle, filled it with PMS 431, a gray shade, and positioned the rectangle over the center of the pamphlet. She placed the bark texture TIFF, which was black, over the gray rectangle and dragged its corner handle to fit. Because the TIFF is transparent, the gray background shows through the clear areas.

9 Adding type

Hewitt typed the pamphlet title in Garamond Light in 36 points with Auto leading and used Garamond Bold Italic in 13/26 points for the University's name. Both elements are reversed with Very Loose Track used to space the letters. She added the publication number on the back, as well as a small white rectangle as an accent on the front cover.

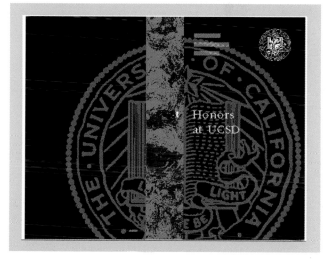

10 Creating a three-color file for output

After on-screen approval of the color file, Hewitt created a second file for spot color separations. The Pantone purple and process tint were respecified as black and 80 percent black to produce one plate to be printed purple. The bark texture was specified blue to produce a plate to be printed in black. The gray rectangle produced the third plate.

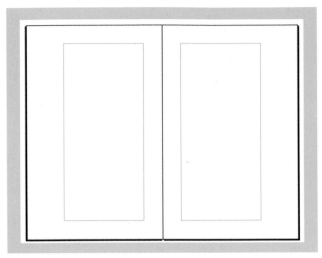

11 Setting up a 1-column grid

To provide a basic framework for the inside pages of the pamphlet, Hewitt specified a page size of 5.5 x 8.75 inches, with facing pages and a single column with deep margins of 0.75 inch inside, at the top, and at the bottom, and 1.5 inches on the outside. The wide outside margin provided white space that makes the design look spacious and uncluttered.

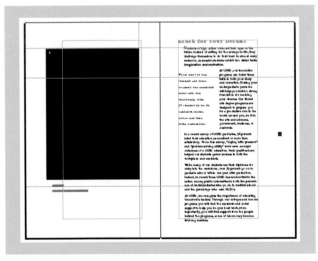

12 Importing text and creating windows for art

The text for the pamphlet was typed in Microsoft Word and imported into PageMaker without formatting. Paragraph styles were applied to the type, which was placed in a single column on each 2-page spread. Black rectangles were created as windows for conventional stripping of duotones into the film; the windows were coded to match the codes marked on the photos.

Why UCSD?

The thought of studying at our campus may be a new one for you. Because UCSD is thirty years young, its history may not be as well known to you as the reputation of some other prestigious schools. Upon closer inspection, however, you'll soon discover that UCSD is making headlines across the nation. In fact, the achievements of our students and faculty prompted *U.S. News and World Report* to select UCSD as one of America's "Up-and-Coming" national universities.

"Although UCSD is best known for science, some of its most interesting and impressive programs are in the humanities and social sciences. Its honors program in literature is the best I've seen."

FRANCES SMITH FOSTER,
PROFESSOR OF LITERATURE

The National Science Foundation has long recognized UCSD as a high-powered research university. In fact, UCSD ranks seventh in the nation for the amount of federal dollars it receives for research and development (1989). Our campus is home base for many organized research units, such as Scripps Institution of Oceanography, the Center for Magnetic Recording Research, the Center for Molecular Genetics, and the Center for U.S.- Mexican Studies. These centers mean not only outstanding faculty, but also research opportunities for our undergraduates.

Of particular note is the San Diego Supercomputer Center, which is based on campus. The center's supercomputer is capable of over 2.7 billion computations per second. Each year our undergraduates successfully compete with the nation's best minds for time on the amazing CRAY computer system.

13 Using variations of 1 typeface

Hewitt used only 1 typeface — Garamond — throughout the pamphlet, but changed its weight, point size, leading, letter spacing, and color to produce variations that help organize and easily distinguish the different parts of the text.

Headlines were set in Garamond Bold, in 12/12 points, flush left, with No Track, in PMS 431. To spread the titles horizontally, Hewitt used the space bar to enter spaces between characters.

Body text was set as Garamond Light, in 9.5/12 point, flush left, with a Normal Track, in black.

An initial cap at the beginning of each block of body text was specified as Garamond Bold 12/12 point.

Pull quotes were set in Garamond Bold Italic with Loose Track. Both styles were set in 9.5/18 point. A credit line at the bottom of each quote was set in Garamond Light, in 9.5/18 and Loose Track to match the size and spread of the quote, but its Small Caps style and its color set the credit off from the quote.

Headlines were set to run flush left with a Left Indent of 0.25 inches to control the start of the second line; to get the first line to start farther left, the First Indent was set at –0.25 inches. ⌘ *In PageMaker's paragraph styles, the first-line indent is measured from the Left Indent setting, so a first-line "outdent" requires a negative setting.*

Body text was assigned a Left Indent of 0.25 inches. Hewitt specified a Space After of 6 points for the body text so that the space between paragraphs would be half of the body text leading of 12 points. The Space After specification, accessed through the Paragraph dialog box, automatically inserts a space whenever the Return key is used to end a paragraph of text.

Poised on the Cutting Edge

Our faculty and their pioneering research are a constant source of pride for the campus. Here are a few of the researchers who are a part of UCSD:

■ One of UCSD's founding fathers, the late **Roger Revelle**, was honored by President George Bush with a National Medal of Science in 1990. The award paid tribute to Revelle's pioneering work in a variety of fields, including global warming and oceanographic exploration. Revelle's presence will be felt on the campus for many years to come.

■ **Michael Schudson**, professor of sociology and communication, received a $270,000 award from the MacArthur Foundation, which will help him continue his research on how culture and the media influence each other. Schudson was named an "Outstanding Teacher" by his undergraduate students.

■ One of the nation's leading AIDS researchers, **Flossie Wong-Staal** (who is also a professor of medicine at UCSD), is making headlines around the globe as she helps crack the mysteries of the disease. Recently, the Institute for Scientific Information named her the most frequently cited woman in science. Several undergraduates have worked alongside Wong-Staal through independent "199" study.

14 Adding boldface and dingbat ornaments

Type styles created in PageMaker are applied to an entire paragraph. So to change type specifications within a paragraph it is necessary to individually select the elements to be changed and apply new specifications. To call attention to the names in a list of well-known faculty, Hewitt selected each name and typed Command-Shift-B to change the type to boldface. She also added 6-point squares from the Zapf Dingbats font to the beginning of each paragraph. This was done by typing a lowercase "n" at the beginning of each paragraph, selecting it, and scrolling through the Font submenu to select the Zapf Dingbats font.

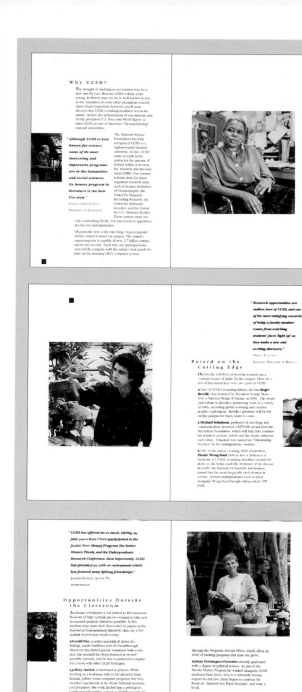

15 Varying the layouts

To vary the look of each page Hewitt placed the blue pull quotes in a different position each time. On some pages the pull quote is flush left in the text column while the text flows around it to the right. On other pages the pull quote is placed at the top of the page, outside the column, with the body text placed below it.

Hewitt was provided with a selection of high-quality black-and-white photographs of students, faculty, and the campus, including 2 by Ansel Adams. She selected 2 photos for each page spread, featured 1 by itself in a square format, and cropped the other to a smaller vertical rectangle, usually to isolate a single person. The photographs were separated as duotones in black and gray, and the printer stripped them into the final film, matching the letter code on each photo with the reverse letter in its upper left corner of the corresponding black window in the layout.

The composition of each page spread was completed by adding a small purple square as an accent. The square appears on each spread in a different place, positioned by Hewitt according to her sense of the dynamics of the spread. Usually the square is aligned to some other element, such as a headline, a block of body text, or 1 of the column guides.

9

Laying Out a Book Cover

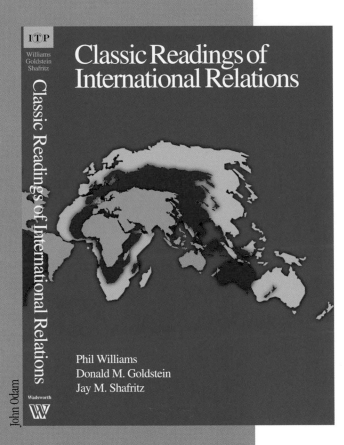

Laying out a book cover requires precision. In PageMaker you can make the spine exactly the right width and position it precisely in the center of the wrap-around cover design, with a minimum of measurement and calculation.

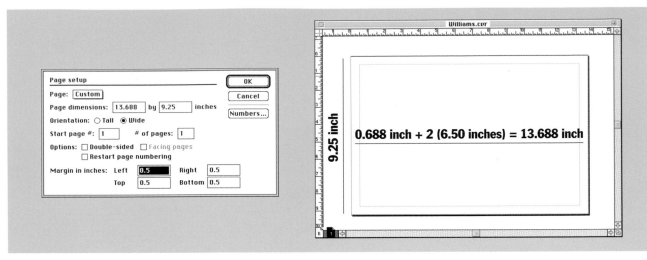

1 Setting up the page size

John Odam began production of his cover design for a college textbook by setting up the entire cover (front, back, and spine) as a single page. The height of the page was the height of the book cover (9.25 inches). The width of the page was the width of the spine plus twice the width of the book (6.50 inches). The spine width is 0.688 inch, a measurement that the printer had computed by multiplying the number of pages in the book by the thickness of a single sheet of paper.

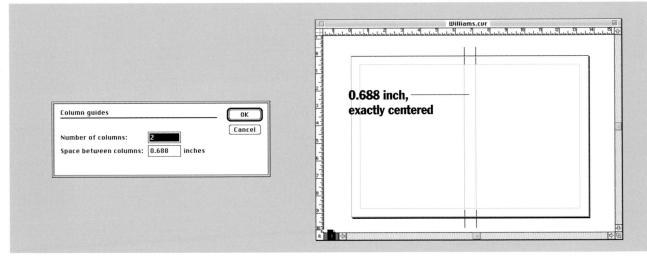

2 Centering the spine

In a book cover design, the spine must be exactly in the center of the wrap-around cover. Rather than relying on his own measurements and calculations, Odam let PageMaker do the work for him automatically. He chose Column Guides from the Options menu and set up a 2-column format. For the Space Between Columns, or gutter, he specified the spine width measurement. PageMaker automatically centered the gutter exactly in the middle of a 2-column page.

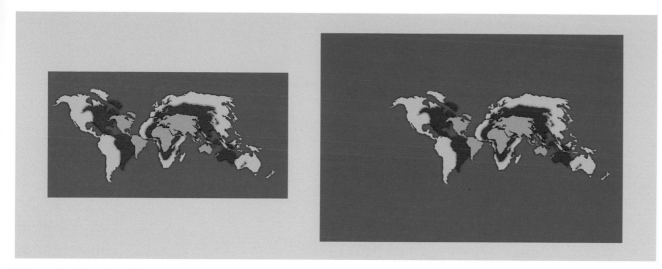

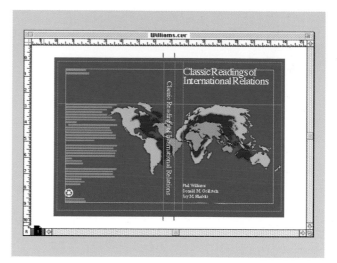

3 Preparing the artwork

Odam prepared a cover illustration in Adobe Photoshop. To speed up his work, he used a file just large enough to hold the layered map. When he had finished the map, he enlarged the blue background enough to cover the entire PageMaker page and to provide a 0.25-inch bleed. ⬤ *When separated and printed, a color created in one program may look different than a color with the same CMYK specifications created in another program.*

4 Using guidelines

Odam dragged horizontal and vertical guidelines from the rulers onto the page to align the type for the title and the authors' names, and to align the top of the text on the back cover with the top of the map. At the top and bottom of the spine, he drew short black lines with the line tool to indicate on proofs where the folds for the spine would be; he sent these lines to the back.

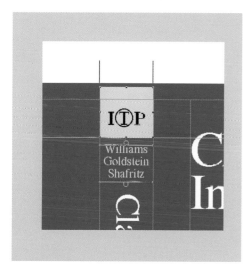

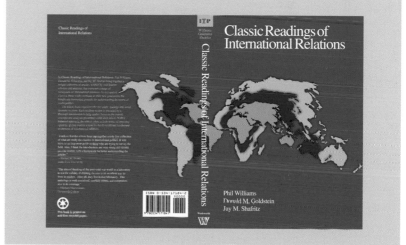

5 Fitting elements to the spine

With the Snap To Guides function turned on, Odam could easily stretch the type block for the authors' names to fit between the guidelines that defined the gutter. The rectangle of color behind the ITP logo also snapped to fit the spine.

6 Creating the bar code

Odam used BarCode Pro, a program that can generate a wide variety of codes — such as ISBN, SKU, and postal code bars — to set the code for the back of the book. BarCode Pro can produce the codes as encapsulated PostScript files (the format Odam used to place the codes in the PageMaker layout) or as PICT graphics.

7 Completing the cover

To complete the PageMaker file, Odam drew a white background rectangle to hold the bar code and added 2 more logos that were required to appear on the cover. The completed cover file, almost 10 x 14 inches and including linked graphics, occupied only 1 MB of disk space. This relatively small size was due mainly to the fact that PageMaker could import the Photoshop artwork, with its large areas of flat color, in TIFF format with LZW compression.

10
Creating an Identity Package

Calvin Woo Associates

PALMILLA

Using only 2 typefaces and elements drawn from a single graphic symbol, designers were able to create a variety of printed materials for a resort hotel in Mexico.

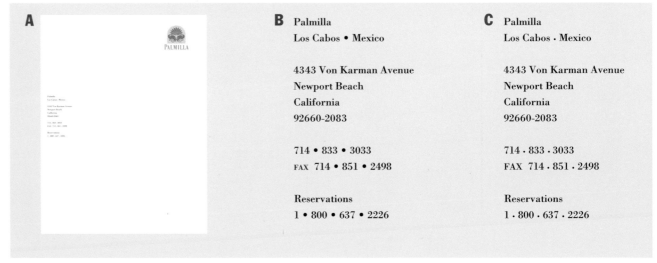

1 Creating a logo and decorative elements

Before they began designing the stationery for Palmilla, a resort hotel in Los Cabos, Mexico, designers Susan Merritt and Calvin Woo of Calvin Woo Associates used Adobe Illustrator to create both the logotype and the graphic symbol for the identity. The type was based on Bodoni, while the graphic was a refined version of a pre-existing symbol. They created a 1-color version in black-and-white (A) and a 2-color version using Pantone colors 320 (turquoise) and 169 (papaya) (B). They also adapted parts of the logo to create decorative elements. For example, they isolated half of the bird design (C) and also created a pattern based on the swirls under the bird, which was used to create a pattern fill in Illustrator (D). The pattern was rendered in several color combinations to provide backgrounds for menus and cards (E).

2 Designing a letterhead sheet

To create a letterhead sheet, the designers opened an 8.5 x 11-inch (letter-size) page in PageMaker, imported the 2-color logo, and positioned it at the upper right corner of the page. They then typed the resort's name, address, and telephone numbers in 8/12-point Bodoni, assigned Pantone 320 to the type, and positioned the text block in the center of the left side of the page (A). The text included bullets between the city and country names and between the elements of the phone numbers. The 8-point bullets looked too large (B), so the designers reduced them to 4-point type, but did not adjust the baseline, so the bullets are positioned slightly below the center of the height of the 8-point characters (C).

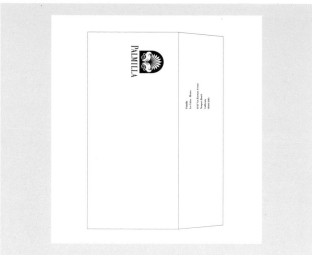

3 Designing an envelope

For a business-size envelope, the designers added a page to the letterhead file and drew the shapes of a 9.5 x 4.25-inch envelope as guides for themselves and the printer. They imported the logo, rotated it –90°, and positioned it. They copied the text block from the letterhead, deleted the telephone numbers, rotated the text block +90°, and positioned it on the flap.

4 Designing a 1-color news sheet

The designers also used Adobe Illustrator to create a 1-color news sheet for press releases from the hotel (the top half is shown here) (C). The news sheet could also have been created in PageMaker by simply setting and positioning type and importing the 1-color logo. The news sheet design was created in black and printed in Pantone 320.

5 Designing a mailing label

Rather than print envelopes in a variety of sizes, the designers created a mailing label that could be attached to ready-made envelopes. The 3.25 x 5.25-inch label was created in PageMaker using the 2-color logo and an address block set in the same 8-point Bodoni used for the letterhead. For the label, however, the leading was reduced from 12 to 11 points.

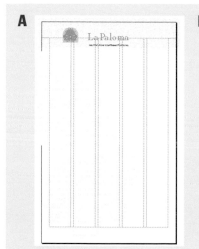

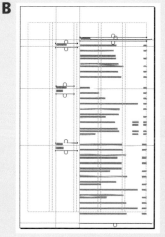

C

DINNER

Appetizers

Steamed Shrimp with Chipotle and Beer	8.50
Scallop Ceviche in Lime and Cilantro	7.75
Charred Pasilla filled with Queso Anejo and Crispy Lamb in a pool of Tomatillos	7.25
Tamale with Potatoes, Chicken, Garbanzos and Olives in a Banana Leaf with Avocado Salsa	6.50
Chilled Shrimp Cocktail with Salsa Fresca	9.50

6 Creating temporary menus

The hotel's restaurant needed new menus quickly, to use until a more permanent version could be printed. The designers used logo elements created in Adobe Illustrator, plus type generated in PageMaker to create a 2-color legal-size sheet that served as a background. The headline at the top was set in 48-point Cochin with a Set Width of 90 percent (A). The designers then set type for the current breakfast, lunch, and dinner menus in a separate PageMaker document and used these to print the menu text onto the printed 2-color sheets using a laser printer (B). The menu type was set in Cochin using 15/18-point in Small Caps for the heads, 11/18-point for the subheads, and 10/12-point type for the entrees (C).

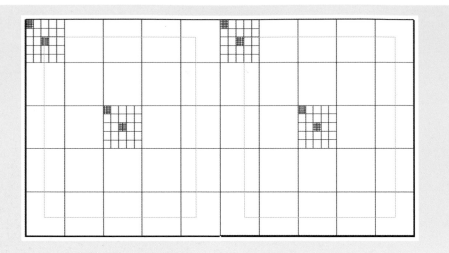

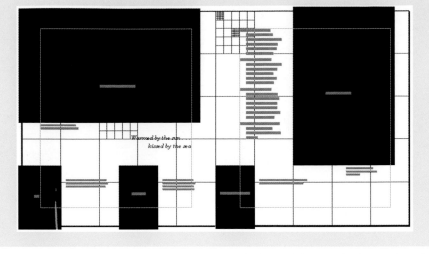

7 Creating master pages for a brochure

To provide a way to organize the many photos and text blocks needed for a full-color promotional brochure, the designers specified 9 x 8-inch pages and used PageMaker's line tool to draw a grid system on the master pages. Each page was divided into 25 vertical rect-angles, and 2 of these were further divided into subunits of 25. The system is called a "grid of fifths."

8 Laying out the brochure

The designers checked Display Master Items from the Page menu so that they could see the grid lines, then fol-lowed both the large (first generation) rectangles and next smaller subdivisions (second generation) to align the type blocks and the horizontal and vertical photo-graphs that would be stripped in later. Each window was labeled in reverse type with the name of the photo to be used. A heading for each 2-page spread was set in 18/21-point Bodoni italic, while captions were set in 7.5/9-point Bodoni. The Display Master Items command was turned off when the layout was ready for output.

*W*armed by the sun . . .
kissed by the sea, the Hotel
Palmilla is praised by
seasoned travelers as the
most enchanting seaside
sanctuary of its kind.

*S*o relax. And get reac-
quainted with someone
you've missed for quite some
time. Yourself.

9 Setting type for body text

To create an open feeling on the spreads, the designers set the body text in 9-point Bodoni with a wide, 14-point leading. An initial cap at the start of each paragraph was set in 12-point Bodoni italic.

10 Printing the brochure

The PageMaker files were output to film and also to paper, to create mechanicals with instruc-tions to the printer. Headlines were marked to be printed in Pantone 320 and the rest of the type in black. The photographs were stripped into the film conventionally and screened-back illustrations of a palm tree, parrot, and turtle were pasted up mechanically and printed behind the type.

11 Creating golf club materials

The covers for an application form, rules book, and score card for the resort's golf club completed the resort's ini-tial identity package.

11

Creating Professional Stationery

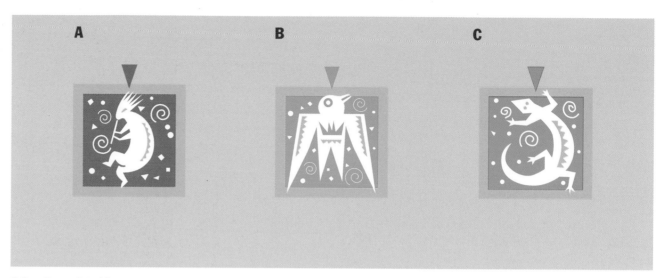

A | B | C

DARLENE | MCELROY
DESIGN & | ILLUSTRATION

3723 BIRCH, SUITE FOURTEEN
NEWPORT BEACH, CA 92660
714 . 434 . 7220

Darlene McElroy

An attractive letterhead system can serve as a sample of a designer's skills. Darlene McElroy used colorful icons, soft backgrounds, a careful type treatment, and recycled paper to create a business card, letter sheet, envelope, and mailing label for her business.

1 Creating related icons

Darlene McElroy began her set of stationery by using Aldus FreeHand to create a group of 3 related 2-color icons, each based on a piece of primitive art and each featuring gold and 1 other spot color. Each of the icons would be used on 1 of the 3 stationery pieces she planned to make: a business card (A), an envelope (B), and a memo-sized sheet (C). The icons are shown here at actual size.

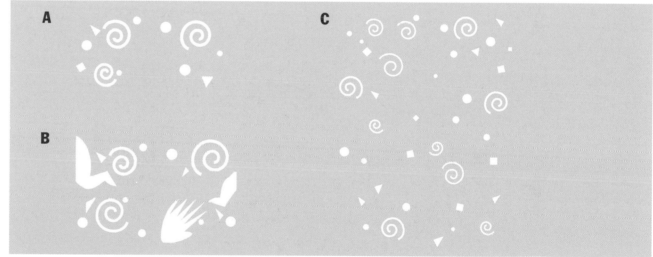

A | C

B

2 Creating backgrounds

McElroy also used FreeHand to create a set of 3 background images, based on the spirals and geometric shapes in the icons. These were assigned a 15% tint of the same gold used in the icons. The backgrounds were created at actual size: 3.5 x 2 inches for the business card (A), 6.5 x 2.5 inches for the envelope flap (B), and 6.25 x 8.5 inches for the letter sheet (C). The backgrounds are shown here at reduced size.

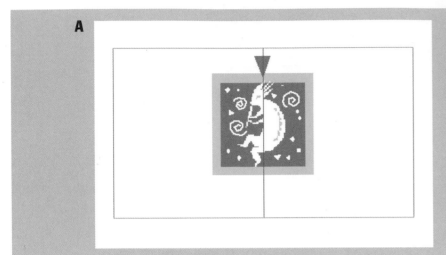

A

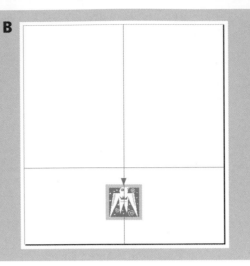

B

C

3 Assembling the elements in PageMaker

Because of the difference in sizes, McElroy created a separate PageMaker document for each of the 3 stationery pieces, each with the page sized exactly to the finished size of the piece. She then imported the FreeHand graphics she had created and positioned them on the pages. The pages were specified with no margins. McElroy used guides to help in centering and positioning the icons. The background for the business card was allowed to bleed off the edge of the page (A). The page for the envelope was sized to its dimensions when the flap is unfolded, 6.5 x 7.25 inches. Then a guide was placed where the fold would lie and the graphic elements were positioned below that, in the area of the flap (B). The icon for the letter sheet was centered 0.25 inches below the top of the page (C).

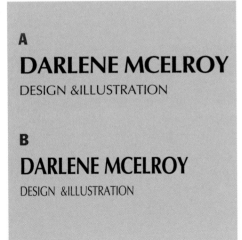

4 Applying Set Width to the type

McElroy set the type for her name in 18-point Optima Bold and specified a Set Width of 80% to condense the type. She set her title in 10-point Optima and specified a Set Width of 75%. The type is shown before (A) and after (B) the Set Width changes.

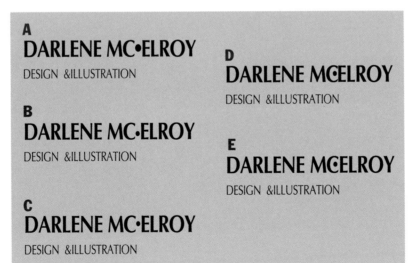

5 Adding an ornament

To separate the 2 parts of her last name, which might otherwise be confusing in all caps, McElroy typed a Helvetica bullet between them (A), reduced its size to 12 points (B), raised its baseline to center it vertically (C), and decreased the letterspace by kerning the bullet (Option-Delete) until it was inside the "C" (D). She then increased the letterspace between the bullet and the "E" by placing the cursor between them and typing Option-Shift-Delete until the letters looked right (E).

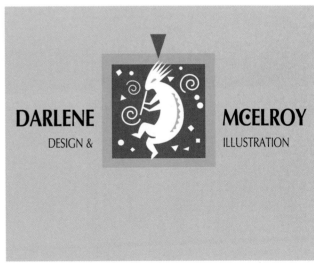

6 Spacing the type around the logo

McElroy positioned the type to the left of the icon on the business card and dragged the text block's right upper handle to the right to spread it across the icon. She placed her cursor between her 2 names, and pressed the Tab key and then the spacebar until the second name was on the right side of the icon. She used the same procedure to move the second half of her title.

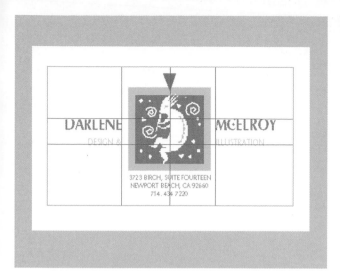

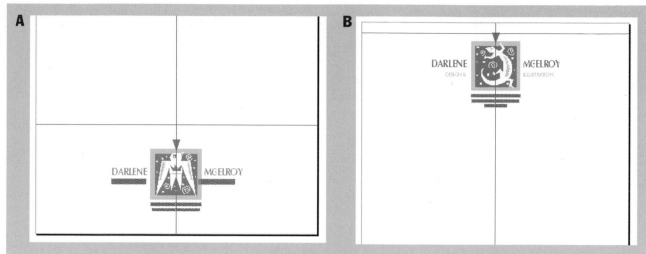

7 Coloring the type to match the business card art

McElroy set her address in 7/8.5-point Optima with a 90% Set Width and Tight track and centered it beneath the icon. She then colored the type with the purple that now appeared in the Colors palette. ⬛ *When EPS graphics containing spot colors (or FreeHand EPS files with either spot or process colors) are imported, the colors appear in PageMaker's Colors palette.*

8 Adding type to the envelope and letter sheet

McElroy selected and copied the finished type elements from the business card file, then opened the envelope file, pasted the type from the clipboard, positioned it around the icon, and changed the color of the purple type to match the blue in the envelope icon (A). She used the same procedures to copy and paste the type into the letter sheet document and changed the color of the type to match the green in the letter sheet icon (B).

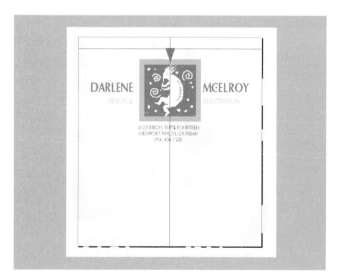

9 Creating a mailing label

Later on, as McElroy's needs changed, she decided to print a mailing label she could use on larger envelopes. Rather than create a new icon, she used the artwork she had made for her business card and adapted the FreeHand background file to fit the new 3.5 x 4-inch size, exactly double the size of the business card.

10 Finishing the stationery

McElroy printed spot separations from her stationery files and specified Pantone colors to match the purple, green, and blue she had created for screen viewing. The gold was printed in a metallic copper color. The stationery pieces were printed on matching sheets, envelopes, and card weight stock made of a beige recycled paper with a soft speckle that complemented the metallic ink.

Janet Ashford

BIRTH HISTORY
POSTCARDS

**A set of 16 images
depicting childbirth in history
$5.00 per set**
Also available as art prints (8 1/2 x 11 inches)
for $15.00 per set

ORDER FROM JANET ISAACS ASHFORD
327 Glenmont Drive
Solana Beach, California 92075

For a mail-order business selling educational materials on the childbirth, a variety of related publications were created, including a postcard set, an art print set, labels, and display ads in several sizes.

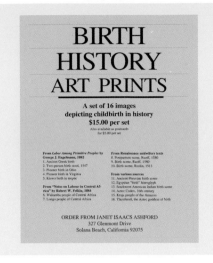

1 Setting type for art prints

To create type for a set of prints on birth history, 2 PageMaker documents were opened; 1 with 6 letter-size pages in Wide format and the other with 10 pages in Tall format, to accommodate the orientations of the images. Type for the image descriptions was set in 9-point Times, with 8-point for a credit line. The type blocks were centered and placed at the bottoms of the pages, which were printed on a laser printer. Conventional black-and-white stats of the artwork were pasted on.

2 Designing a package label

The sets of prints were packaged in manila envelopes with a letter-size label. Type for the labels was set in Times in point sizes from 90 down to 12, all with Loose track. Horizontal rules and a border helped to organize the page, which was laser-printed on colored paper.

A

B

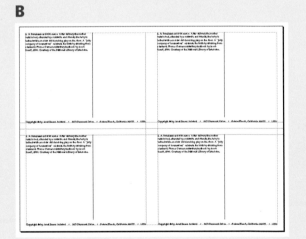

3 Setting up 4-up postcard layouts

A set of 16 postcards matching the prints was planned so that 4 could be cut from a single 8.5 x 11-inch sheet of card-weight stock, glossy on one side. For the text on the back side, the PageMaker page was specified with 0.25-inch margins all around and 2 columns with a 0.5-inch space between the columns. Horizontal guides were placed at the center of the page and at 0.25 inches above and below the center, dividing the page into 4 equal rectangles, each with a 0.25-inch margin. Text for a card description and credit line was set in 8-point Times with Auto leading. The text and a vertical rule dividing the message and address areas of the postcard were positioned in the upper left rectangle of the page (A). These elements were copied and positioned in the other rectangles (B), and each new description was typed over the old.

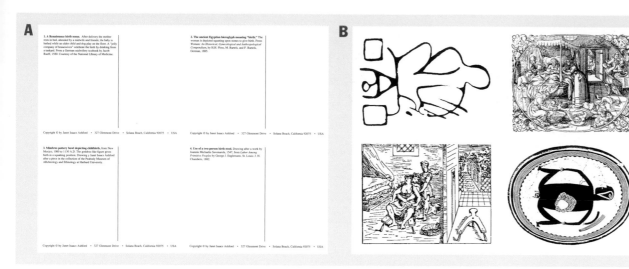

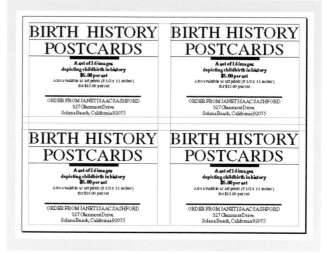

4 Preparing mechanicals for the printer

The finished postcard text document was laser printed on hard-surfaced white paper at 300 dpi and supplied to the printer as copy for making plates (A). Art for the cards was output as conventional stats and positioned on another 8.5 x 11-inch sheet to correspond with the positions of the card text (B). In all, 4 sets of text and art mechanicals were required to produce 16 postcards.

5 Designing postcard labels

To create labels for the postcard sets, the document used for the postcard text was saved under a new name and the same guides were used for positioning the label text, which was set in Times in a style similar to that used for the prints label. The labels were printed on 8.5 x 11-inch sheets of colored paper and cut into 4.25 x 5.5-inch labels (see opening art).

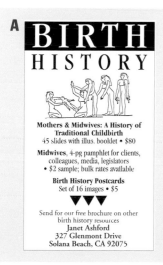

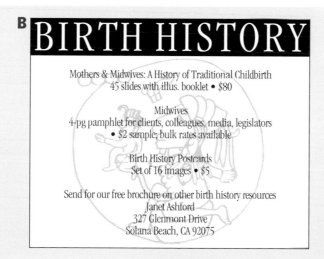

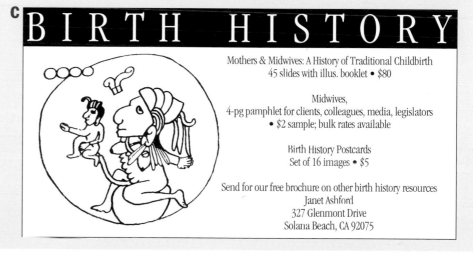

6 Creating display ads

Display advertisements in a variety of formats were created for placement in magazines dealing with childbirth. Most magazines employ a 3-column format, with 2.25-inch wide columns. A 1-column ad was prepared at this width, using a graphic and type set in a condensed face, Garamond Light Condensed, to get as much text into the narrow width as possible (A). A 2-column ad was created at a 4.75-inch width to fit 2 magazine columns plus the 0.25-inch space between them. An imported graphic with 30% black applied was used behind the type (B). A 3-column version at a width of 7.25 inches included the same graphic used in black on the left and the descriptive text on the right (C). For readers who encounter the 3 advertisements in different publications, the use of the same reversed headline in all 3 ads helps to identify them as coming from the same source. The reversed type was spread evenly across the black bars by specifying an alignment of Force Justify and by using the space bar to enter a space between each pair of letters and 2 spaces between words.

13

Designing a Mail-Order Brochure

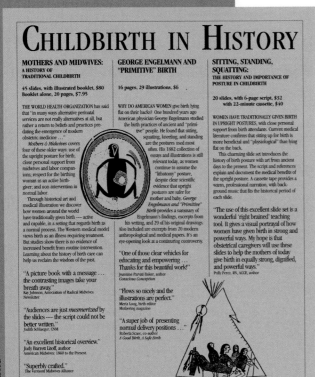

Janet Ashford

CHILDBIRTH IN HISTORY

MOTHERS AND MIDWIVES:
A HISTORY OF
TRADITIONAL CHILDBIRTH

45 slides, with illustrated booklet, $80
Booklet alone, 20 pages, $7.95

THE WORLD HEALTH ORGANIZATION has said that "in many ways alternative perinatal services are not really alternatives at all, but rather a return to beliefs and practices pre-dating the emergence of modern obstetric medicine . . ."

Mothers & Midwives covers four of these older ways: use of the upright posture for birth; close personal support from midwives and labor companions; respect for the birthing woman as an active birth-giver; and non-intervention in normal labor.

Through historical art and medical illustration we discover how women around the world have traditionally given birth — active and capable, in a setting that regards birth as a normal process. The Western medical model views birth as an illness requiring treatment. But studies show there is no evidence of increased benefit from routine intervention. Learning about the history of birth care can help us reclaim the wisdom of the past.

"A picture book with a message . . . the contrasting images take your breath away."
Kay Johnson, Association of Radical Midwives Newsletter

"Audiences are just *mesmerized* by the slides — the script could not be better written."
Judith Schlaeger, CNM

"An excellent historical overview."
Judy Barrett Litoff, author
American Midwives: 1860 to the Present.

"Superbly crafted."
The Vermont Midwives Alliance

GEORGE ENGELMANN AND "PRIMITIVE" BIRTH

16 pages, 29 illustrations, $6

WHY DO AMERICAN WOMEN give birth lying flat on their backs? One hundred years ago American physician George Engelmann studied the birth practices of ancient and "primitive" people. He found that sitting, squatting, kneeling, and standing are the postures used most often. His 1882 collection of essays and illustrations is still relevant today, as women continue to assume the "lithotomy" posture, despite clear scientific evidence that upright postures are safer for mother and baby. *George Engelmann and "Primitive" Birth* provides a summary of Engelmann's findings, excerpts from his writing, and 29 of his original drawings. Also included are excerpts from 20 modern anthropological and medical papers. It's an eye-opening look at a continuing controversy.

"One of those clear vehicles for educating and empowering . . . Thanks for this beautiful work!"
Jeannine Parvati Baker, author
Conscious Conception

"Flows so nicely and the illustrations are perfect."
Merita Gong, birth editor
Mothering magazine

"A super job of presenting normal delivery positions . . ."
Roberta Scaer, co-author
A Good Birth, A Safe Birth

SITTING, STANDING, SQUATTING:
THE HISTORY AND IMPORTANCE OF POSTURE IN CHILDBIRTH

20 slides, with 6-page script, $32
with 22-minute cassette, $40

WOMEN HAVE TRADITIONALLY GIVEN BIRTH IN UPRIGHT POSTURES, with close personal support from birth attendants. Current medical literature confirms that sitting up for birth is more beneficial and "physiological" than lying flat on the back.

This charming slide set introduces the history of birth posture with art from ancient days to the present. The script and references explain and document the medical benefits of the upright posture. A cassette tape provides a warm, professional narration, with background music that fits the historical period of each slide.

"The use of this excellent slide set is a wonderful 'right brained' teaching tool. It gives a visual portrayal of how women have given birth in strong and powerful ways. My hope is that obstetrical caregivers will use these slides to help the mothers of today give birth in equally strong, dignified, and powerful ways."
Polly Perez, RN, ACCE, author

• CHILDBIRTH RESOURCES BY JANET ISAACS ASHFORD •

A simple 3-column structure, a single typeface in several sizes and weights, and graphics drawn from the mail-order products described in the preceding chapter were used to create a brochure with order form.

1 Creating a framework for a product brochure

To create a brochure that describes the childbirth literature available from a mail-order business, an 8.5 x 11-inch page was specified with 3 columns. A title was set in 77-point Garamond Condensed Light, a hairline border and rules were drawn, and a reversed subtitle was set in 18-point Garamond Condensed Light and placed in a black bar.

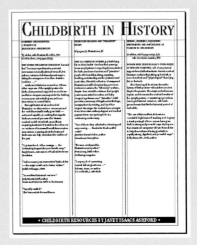

2 Setting type

Text for the brochure included the titles of the publications, their prices and number of pages, a description, and quotes from reviews. The first step in constructing the layout was to enter all the text, styled as body text, in 11/12-point Garamond Book Condensed. One column was devoted to each product, with 3 products on the front of the sheet (shown) and 3 on the back.

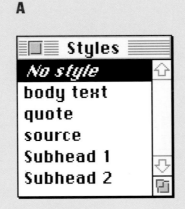

3 Creating type styles

To accommodate later changes to the text, 5 styles were created in the Styles menu, all using Garamond Condensed: "body text" for the descriptions, "quote" for the reviews (14/14-point), "source" for the reviewers (9/9-point), "Subhead 1" for the product titles (16/16-point, All Caps, Bold), and "Subhead 2" for the product prices and parameters (11/12-point, Bold) (A). The styles were applied to each of the different parts of the text (B).

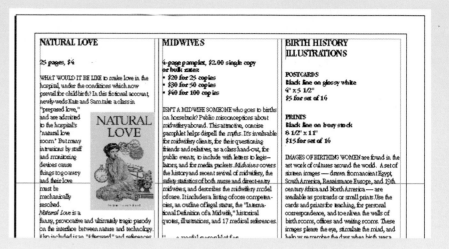

4 Styling and adjusting the type

Because the product titles and parameters varied in length, the product descriptions began at different depths. Titles were set in Subhead 1 style (16/16-point Garamond Book Condensed bold in All Caps) and prices and other parameters were set in Subhead 2 (same font in 11/12 points). The leading between typed lines was sometimes adjusted up or down a few points to make sure the baselines of the product description text aligned horizontally across the pages.

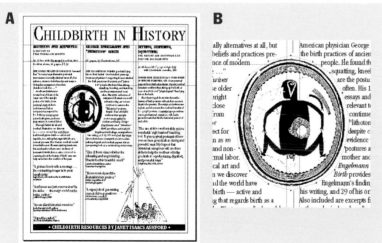

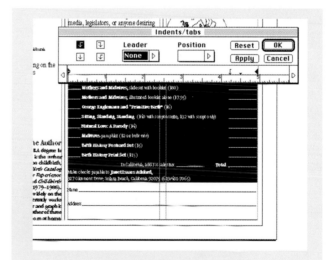

5 Adding graphics

Scans of 2 historical childbirth images were positioned on the front of the brochure (A). A text wrap was applied to the image at the upper left and the wrap boundary was adjusted to the oval graphic so that the text flowed in smooth curves around it (B).

6 Adding an order form

To create an order form for the back of the brochure, product names were typed in 10-point Garamond Condensed Light with wide, 18-point leading and the underscore key was used to type rules. The Indents/Tabs command was used to set up a tab to start the rule at the end of each line of type. The lines for name and address were specified with 26-point leading.

7 Finishing the brochure back

Two scanned graphics were positioned on the back of the brochure and text wraps were applied to both of them. The brochure was printed on colored paper (see opening art).

14

Designing a Continuing Series

Payson R. Stevens, Patrick Howell, Leonard Sirota, and Eric Altson

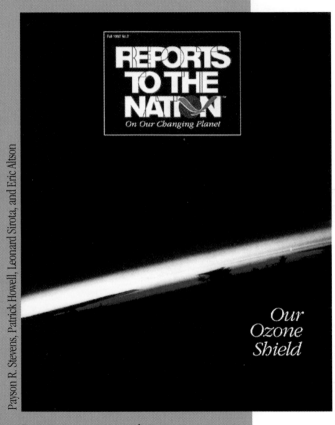

Designers at InterNetwork, Inc. use PageMaker files with full-color illustrations in place to design layouts. But final output is done from files with only type and keylines in place. The resin-coated paper output is pasted up as mechanicals.

1 Designing a publication format

For *Reports to the Nation on Our Changing Planet,* a periodical publication of the University Corporation for Atmospheric Research's Office for Interdisciplinary Studies and the Office of Global Programs of the National Oceanic and Atmospheric Administration (NOAA), designers at InterNetwork, Inc. employ an inviting format that promises to put the reader at ease with the somewhat technical material presented in the *Report.* Spreads from the first 2 issues in the series — "The Climate System" (the "A" examples on these 2 pages) and "Our Ozone Shield" (the "B" examples) — show the pacing of the *Reports.* The inside front cover is both title page and table of contents. Completing the spread is a repeat of the cover photo and a paragraph in white type on a black background that introduces the issue's topic.

2 Using a photo montage

The second spread in each *Report* is a montage of photos and photo-like graphics, some of which may be used elsewhere in the issue (A, B). Like all photos in the publication, these are film transparencies, color-separated and stripped in by traditional means. (Low-resolution desktop scans are used as placeholders for the PageMaker layout.) Another paragraph of white type on black, like the one on the previous spread, continues the process of leading the reader into the publication. In the second issue of the *Reports,* "Our Ozone Shield," the photo montage was presented in the form of a puzzle, with the puzzle-piece outlines created in Aldus FreeHand — once in black for shadows and once in white for highlights.

A

B

3 Beginning the report

The third spread in *Reports to the Nation* includes a full-page graphic that represents the topic of the report. The graphic is output separately from the PageMaker file and stripped into the final film negatives by the printer. For example, the cloud illustration in the first issue (A) was output from Adobe Photoshop, where it was created, through a film recorder as a 4 x 5-inch

transparency, enlarged and separated by a color separation service, and stripped into the film for the pages. The illustration for the second issue (B) was drawn in FreeHand and output directly from an imagesetter as separated film. On the facing page of the spread, the graphic is continued in the form of a "skeletal" line drawing, produced in FreeHand. The title appears on this page, and an initial capital introduces the text.

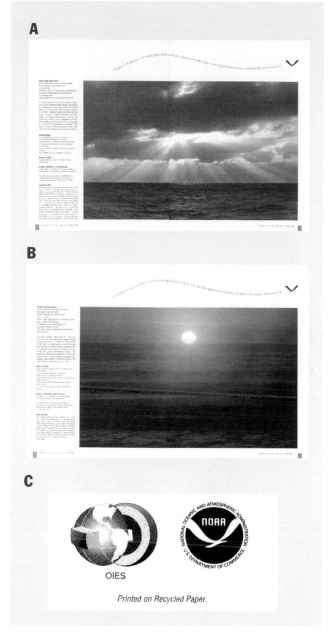

A

B

C

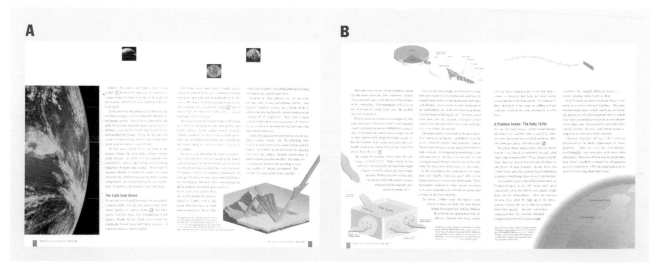

A

B

4 Continuing the story

The fourth and all following spreads in the body of the *Report* incorporate text, photos, imported graphics, captions, and imported type treatments (A, B). Since in most cases the page spreads are built around the graphics, pages are often "roughed-out" by hand and then in FreeHand before the PageMaker pages are constructed. After pages are produced using the tech-

niques described in the next 4 pages, the publication is printed on light gray, slightly textured stock. The type and the background behind reverse text are printed in black, and the graphics are printed in full color. The rectangles behind the page numbers and imported line art and type treatments are printed in a medium-dark gray, created as a black screen stripped in by the printer.

5 Concluding the *Reports*

The last page and the inside back cover include the masthead, photo credits, a photo that crosses the spread, a curving line of type that reiterates a major challenge presented in the issue, and the bird in flight from the NOAA logo (A, B). The back cover includes only logos and the recycled paper notice (C).

A

B

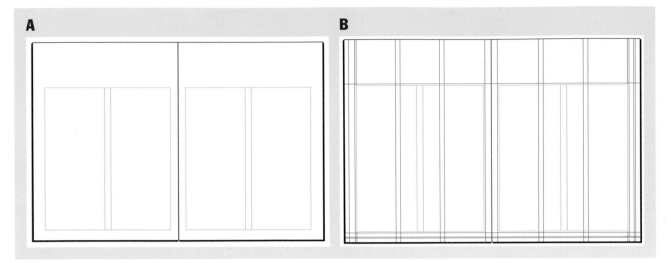

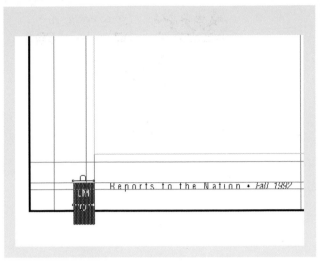

6 Setting up columns and guidelines

Layout of *Reports to the Nation* begins with a template file. The template is set up with a large top margin and 2 columns established on the master pages, with an 8.5 mm gutter between (A). Superimposed on this grid are guidelines to define 3 columns, which can be used for setting the occasional wide or narrow text column needed in the publication (B). Additional guidelines are provided for alignment of elements on the pages, such as folios and running feet.

7 Setting up the folios

A "running foot" on each master page includes the name and date of the publication. A rectangle that bleeds off the page is positioned to hold the page number. ❖ *Automatic page numbering can be added by clicking with the text tool and pressing Command-Option -p.*

A

Ozone molecules show different character traits depending on where they exist in the atmosphere. About 90 percent of the ozone resides in a layer between 10 and 40 kilometers (6 and 25 miles) above the Earth's surface in a region of the atmosphere called the stratosphere. Ozone there plays a beneficial role by absorbing dangerous ultraviolet radiation from the sun. This is the ozone threatened by some

C

Our Ozone Layer: Present and Future

B

But many pieces of the ozone puzzle remain missing, and scientists wonder whether new ozone problems will develop in the near future. Experts are exploring several unanswered questions, including:

D

After it was hypothesized that CFCs could destroy ozone, researchers focused on quantifying this theory. Some hoisted instruments into the stratosphere with huge balloons. Others probed the inner workings of the ozone-destroying chemical reactions in the laboratory. Still others crafted all of this information into computer models, which foretold mounting ozone losses if CFC usage continued to grow.

8 Specifying type

The type for the *Reports* is styled in 2 families of typefaces — Garamond and Helvetica. Twelve-point Garamond type on 18-point leading provides consistent type "color" and good readability in both the wide text column on the opening page (A) and the narrower columns in the body of the publication (B). Garamond, in its italic style, is also used for the title. Subheads (C) and captions (D) appear in 14/18 Helvetica Condensed Bold and 7/9 Helvetica Condensed, respectively.

A   B

Our Ozone Shield   *Our Ozone Shield*

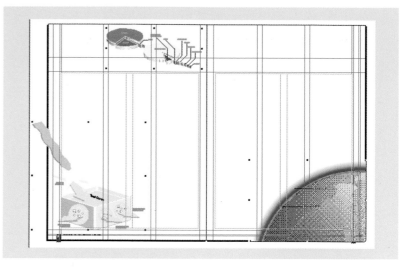

9 Varying the spacing of the type

When necessary, the designers adjust the spacing and character width of display type slightly. For example, positive kerning was used to set the title for "Our Ozone Shield" as it appeared over the table of contents (A), and negative kerning and a Set Width setting of 97% were used when the title appeared on the opening page (B).

10 Importing the large illustrations

Graphics that have been created at full size in Aldus FreeHand and exported as EPS files are placed on the PageMaker spreads. ◆ *The Preferences dialog box offers 3 options for viewing imported graphics: You can choose Gray Out to hold position but to show no detail; this reduces the time it takes for the program to redraw the screen image. Or choose High for the best representation of detail but slow screen refresh, or Normal for a compromise.*

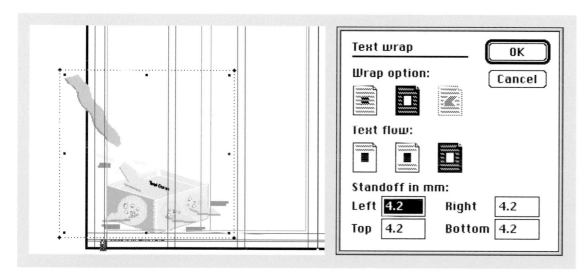

11 Creating a text-wrap border

Each imported illustration is selected and given a boundary that will repel text, by choosing Text Wrap from the Element menu and selecting the middle Wrap Option icon. The InterNetwork designers set a 4.2 mm stand-off distance in the Text Wrap dialog box.

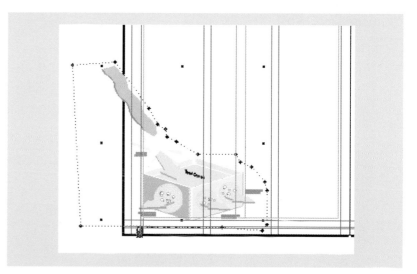

12 Adjusting the wrapping border

Next the border is adjusted to fit the angles and contours of the illustration. ◆ *New anchor points for a text-wrapping border can be created by clicking on the border. Once the point is established, you can drag to change its position. To delete a point, drag it to a neighboring point and release the mouse button.*

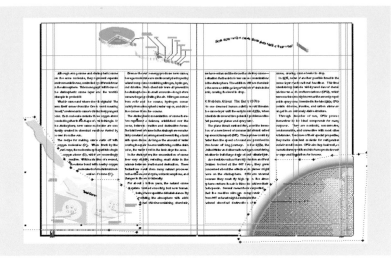

A

odor. Each molecule contains three oxygen atoms bonded together in the shape of a wide triangle. In the stratosphere, new ozone molecules are constantly created in chemical reactions fueled by power from the sun.

The recipe for making ozone starts off with oxygen molecules (O_2). When struck by the sun's rays, the mol-

B

odor. Each molecule contains three oxygen atoms bonded together in the shape of a wide triangle. In the stratosphere, new ozone molecules are constantly created in chemical reactions fueled by power from the sun.

The recipe for making ozone starts off with oxygen molecules (O_2). When struck by the sun's rays, the molecules split apart into single oxygen atoms (O), which are exceedingly reactive. Within a fraction of a second, the atoms bond with nearby oxygen

13 Placing text

The writers supply text as Microsoft Word documents. These files are placed in the PageMaker layout. As the text flows in, it is automatically repelled by the wrapping boundaries of the illustrations. Final adjustments to the wrap are made with the text in place. ● *To keep the text from rewrapping each time a text-wrap border point is moved, hold down the spacebar while you adjust several points, and then release it to see the results.*

14 Inserting inline graphics

One of the elements used by InterNetwork designers to draw the reader's eye to particular points in the text are small line drawings created in FreeHand and placed within the text by clicking with the text tool to establish the insertion point and then choosing File, Place and clicking on As Inline Graphic (A). The graphic is resized and its position is then adjusted with the selection tool to fit within the text leading (B).

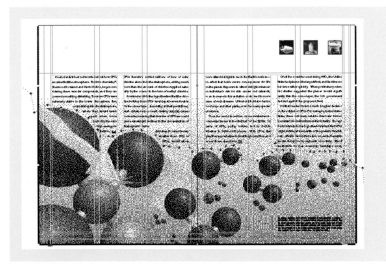

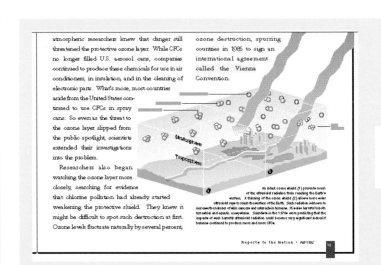

Show layout problems:
☒ **Loose/tight lines**
☒ **"Keeps" violations**

15 Managing large illustration files

FreeHand drawings are generally imported in finished form (see step 10), but large bitmapped illustrations, such as the 2-page-wide molecular diagram on pages 8 and 9 of the second issue of *Reports,* are often several megabytes in size and can be cumbersome to use for layout purposes. The molecule image, created in a 3D program and finished in Photoshop, was saved at full resolution (for output to film) and in a lower-resolution form for placement in the PageMaker file.

16 Checking for layout problems

When text has been placed and wrapped, the InterNetwork designers turn on both options in the Layout Problems section of the Preferences dialog box, so that PageMaker will highlight lines that violate either the specifications for Keep Lines Together in the Paragraph Specifications dialog box (to keep each subhead with the paragraph that follows it) or the word spacing and letter- spacing settings in the Spacing Attributes dialog box (to keep spacing from getting too loose or too tight). With problem areas highlighted in yellow, the designers can decide, on a case-by-case basis, whether to adjust the layout or edit the text slightly.

How does such a small piece play such a huge role?

For millennia, ozone abundances varied naturally, but recently a downward trend has started.

What's causing the ozone hole?

17 Importing type elements

Although PageMaker provides excellent typographic controls, some type treatments are better accomplished in another program and imported. For example, the *Reports to the Nation* nameplate was created in Aldus FreeHand by converting type to outlines and overlapping the letters. The subhead and graphic logo are included in the FreeHand file. For each new issue, the color treatment of the letters can be changed. The nameplate is then exported from FreeHand as an EPS file.

18 Importing type on a path

Another type treatment that cannot be achieved in PageMaker is type on a path. So when the InterNetwork designers wanted to set type in the shape of a hole or use type on a path to visually represent a downward trend, the type was set in FreeHand, exported as an EPS file, and placed in PageMaker as an independent graphic.

ZONE AND HUMANKIND. For nearly a billion ye in the atmosphere have safeguarded life over the past half century, humans have layer in jeopardy. We have unwittingly p chemicals that threaten to eat away the lif surrounding our world.

Although ozone molecules play such a vital rol they are exceedingly rare; in every million molecu ten are ozone Nitrogen and oxygen make up th

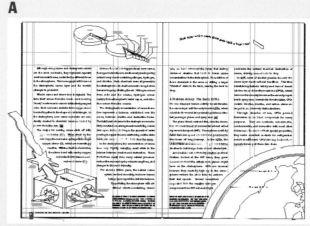

A

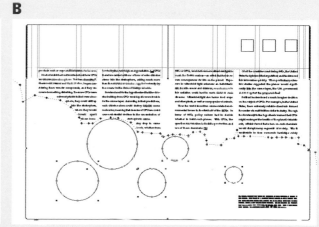

B

19 Importing initial caps

The initial capital is also imported type. The "O" for the "Our Ozone Shield" issue was condensed in FreeHand, exported as an EPS, and placed in Page-Maker as an independent graphic so text could be wrapped around it. ◆ *To wrap text around type set in PageMaker, draw a Paper-colored rectangle or oval behind it and adjust the wrap of this invisible graphic.*

20 Making keyline files

When the layouts are complete, the PageMaker files are "slimmed down" for efficient output and for the printer's ease of use. The PageMaker file is saved under a new name that includes the word "key." Copies of the original FreeHand graphics files are also saved, and the graphics in these new FreeHand files are assigned a 0.5-point black line and white fill. These files

are exported in EPS format and are brought into the "key" file to replace the color illustrations (A). This is done by choosing Element, Link Info and linking the new keyline version; the original text wrap remains in place. For the large bitmapped molecules illustration (see step 15), a copy of the Photoshop file was turned white and linked to the PageMaker file; several "landmark" molecules were drawn as circles in PageMaker (B).

15

Designing a Magazine

Hopkins-Baumann

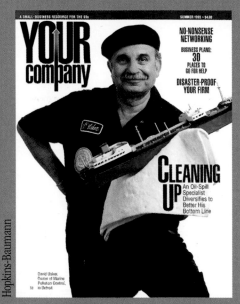

Your Company is a quarterly magazine that goes to American Express cardholders who are entrepreneurs or are otherwise involved in small business ventures. Hopkins-Baumann art directors have designed the magazine to provide readers with information they can use in an easily accessible form.

1 Designing the cover

The editorial goal, and thus also the design goal, of *Your Company* magazine is to deliver useful, interesting information to its million-and-a-half readers, who have no time to waste. The cover of each issue is built around a photo of the subject of the main feature, a businessperson drawn from the readership. Hopkins-Baumann uses the talents of top-notch photographers to produce a high-quality, rock-star-style portrait, with small props and a white background.

2 Varying the nameplate

The simple type-based nameplate announces the magazine's direct, no-nonsense editorial approach. The nameplate was created in Aldus FreeHand and exported in EPS format. The color gradation within the arrow can be changed in FreeHand (and a new EPS made) from issue to issue.

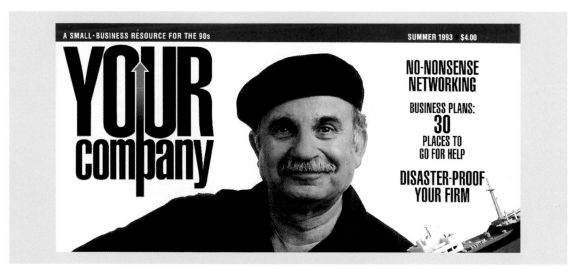

3 Building the cover

A color band at the top of the cover carries the subtitle, "A Small-Business Resource for the 90s." The designers build each cover layout around a low-resolution (72 dpi) scan of the photo. The type is from a single family — Helvetica. By varying the weight and style and mixing caps, small caps, and lower case, the designers integrate the type slugs into the cover.

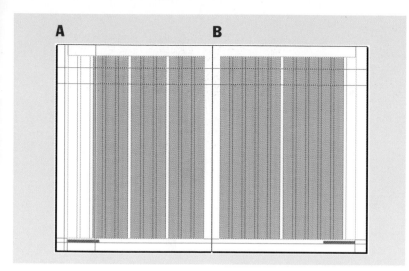

4 Using a flexible grid

The pages of *Your Company* are based on an 11-column grid set up on the master pages. This provides the designers with options that will accommodate a number of page designs based on 3 text columns (using 9 of the original 11) (A) or 2 text columns (of 5 of the original columns each) (B).

5 Designing the table of contents

The table of contents presents the 7 departments, the cover story, another profile article, an article with a psychological slant, an "everything you always wanted to know about . . ." article, and any other editorial content. The nameplate tops the masthead.

6 Importing department logos

The 7 departments are announced by simple, bright logos imported as EPS files from Aldus FreeHand. Shown here are the logos for "Wealth Building" (A) and "Legal Matters" (B).

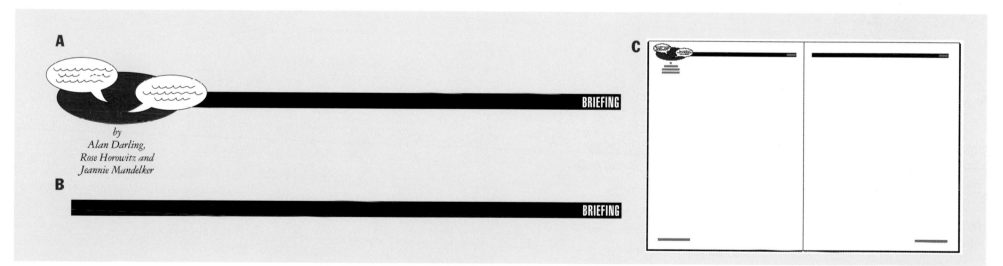

7 Styling department pages

A department logo appears on each left page of the department spreads with a black bar and flush right reverse type that names the department (A). On each right page the bar and reverse type are repeated, but without the logo (B). Producing each department as a separate file provides a set of master pages for each one. The logo, bars, and reverse type are placed on the master pages (C). Then Display Master Items is selected on each page of the department file, so the column identifiers appear on the proper pages, but there is no danger of knocking them out of place while placing text and graphics.

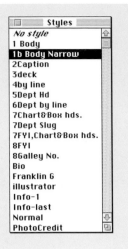

8 Defining type styles

In keeping with the overall style of the magazine, only 3 families of typefaces are used: Garamond, Helvetica, and Franklin Gothic. The most-often-used paragraph styles have names that start with numbers so they appear at the top of the listing in the Style palette.

9 Assembling rough layouts

To plan each issue, the Hopkins-Baumann art directors meet with an editorial team from American Express and with the editor of the magazine to discuss editorial content, illustration, and photography. When the editors have assigned, collected, and edited the columns and articles, they provide the copy to Hopkins-Baumann on disk. Rough illustrations, which arrive on disk or as sketches on paper or by fax or modem, are scanned if necessary and placed in the PageMaker layouts. Line art is scanned at 72 dpi in black-and-white and saved as bitmapped TIFFs (A); other illustrations, as well as photos, are saved as 72 dpi grayscale TIFFs (B). Rough layouts presented to the editorial group at American Express include scans of the final photos, edited text, and rough illustrations; everything that will be in the final layout is shown in context (C).

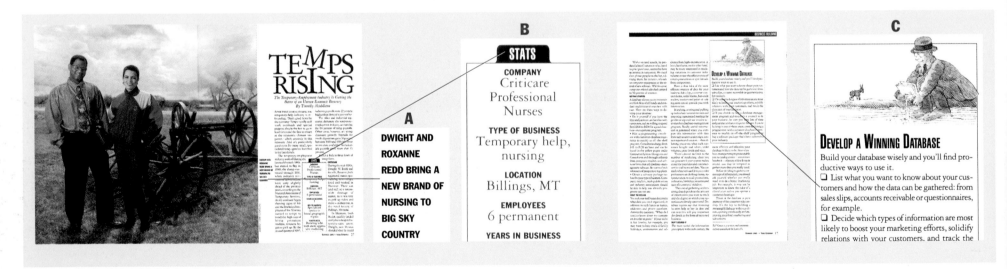

10 Designing with type

In keeping with the editorial goals of the magazine, the designers avoid tints and intricate type wraps, choosing instead to keep the pages clean and straightforward. The body text is 11/12 Garamond 3. Short captions for photos and informational graphics are set flush left in 7.5/12 Franklin Gothic Condensed (A). The "Stats" box, which includes a brief presentation of information about the business featured in the article, serves as both an "executive summary" and a pull quote to draw readers into the article. The "Stats" box is assembled from centered type (6.5-point Franklin Gothic Condensed for the headings and 11/10.5 Garamond 3 for the text), a box defined by a 0.5-point rule and assigned a stand-off to repel the text of the main body copy, and a heading designed to look like an index tab (imported as an EPS file) (B). In addition to body text, the designers use boxed sidebars, often with bulleted lists designed to look like checklists, with a Zapf Dingbats "q" used to provide a drop-shadowed "ballot box" (C).

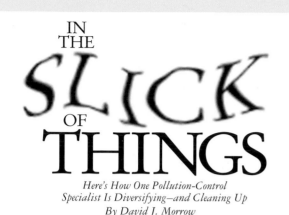

IN THE
Slick
OF
THINGS

Here's How One Pollution-Control
Specialist Is Diversifying—and Cleaning Up
By David J. Morrow

ONE MAN
BANDS

How Solo Operators
Harmonize Autonomy and
Loneliness
By
Barbara B. Buchholz and
Margaret Crane

TEMPS
RISING

The Temporary-Employment Industry Is Getting the
Better of an Uneven Economic Recovery
By Timothy Middleton

11 Designing the article titles

Again, relying on the photos, illustrations, and straightforward typography, the Hopkins-Baumann designers build the article titles using Garamond type. Much of the typesetting is carried out in PageMaker, but some treatments must be imported. For the cover article on a pollution-control specialist, the word "Slick" was modified with a distortion filter in Adobe Photoshop, saved as a grayscale TIFF, and imported into PageMaker. The title for the "One-Man Bands" article (about the stresses of running a one-person business) reinforces the "balancing act" concept illustrated by Ronald Searle (see step 9), with the line length expanding from the byline up. The title for an article about temporary-employment businesses spanned the text columns on the first page, with the "I" enlarged and appearing to displace the "M" to indicate a rise. The type was set in FreeHand, exported as an EPS, and placed in PageMaker. The subtitle and byline were centered under the title; again, this "base" narrowed with each descending line, adding to the sense of growth. ● *Unlike previous versions, PageMaker 5 allows rotation of text to any angle; text can be rotated freely with the rotation tool or by specifying an angle in the Control palette.*

A
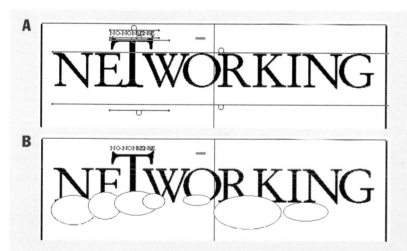

C

D

For the Summer 1993 issue, the subject of the "everything you always wanted to know about . . ." article was networking. Working with a large illustration by Rick Meyerowitz, the designers integrated the title by setting the main word in Garamond 3 type at 163 points, with the "T" set at 230 points; the words "No Nonsense" were then set at 20 points, supported by the bar of the "T" (A). PageMaker's oval tool was used to draw shapes with no line and a

Paper fill on top of the conversation balloons that overlapped the type (the balloons are shown here in red and without the illustration) (B). The shapes blocked out portions of the type to integrate the title with the illustration. The subtitle and byline were placed below the illustration so the type didn't show through the bitmapped scan when the file was viewed on screen or laser-printed (C). They also served as a guide for the printer in assembling the ele-

ments of the page (D). The pages of the magazine are output as laser prints to key the photos and illustrations for placement by the printer. The files are then output on resin-coated paper for a final proofreading before film is output and sent to the printer so that photos and other artwork can be stripped in. Hopkins-Baumann art directors for *Your Company* are Will Hopkins and Mary K. Baumann; designers are Joseph Lee and Angela Esposito.

16
Creating Initial Caps

Initial capital letters, called "initial caps" for short, are the enlarged letters that begin a paragraph and provide extra graphic punch. To enliven pages and draw attention to the text, you can create initial caps within PageMaker, or import the decorative letters from other programs.

A Error is just as important a condition of life as truth.
— C. G. Jung

B Error is just as important a condition of life as truth.
— C. G. Jung

C Error is just as important a condition of life as truth.
— C. G. Jung

Creating a standard raised cap

A *raised initial cap* is taller than the rest of the paragraph it begins, but has the same baseline. The easiest way to create a raised cap is to select the first letter of a paragraph and increase its point size. We started with 10-point Palatino (A) and increased the initial cap to 24 points (B). You can also change the font to contrast with the body type. We used Helvetica Black (C).

F Great music is a psychical storm, agitating to fathomless depths the mystery of the past within us.

Or we might say that it is a prodigious incantation. There are tones that call up all ghosts of youth and joy and tenderness: —there are tones that evoke all phantom pains of perished passion; — there are tones that revive all dead sensations of majesty and might and glory, — all expired exultations, —all forgotten magnanimities.
— Paul Elmer More, 1864–1937

When you include more than 1 initial cap in a text column, be sure to separate the paragraphs with line spaces in the same leading as the body text so that the text is aligned across the columns (F). This example uses 10-point text with 12-point leading and 18-point initial caps. One line space at 12-point leading was inserted between the paragraphs.

D The only thing that makes one place more attractive to me than another is the quantity of *heart* I find in it.
— Jane Welsh Carlyle, 1829

E The only thing that makes one place more attractive to me than another is the quantity of *heart* I find in it.
— Jane Welsh Carlyle, 1829

When Auto leading is specified in a text block, increasing the point size of the first letter will also increase the leading applied to that line (D). To avoid this, select the entire paragraph and specify a single leading value in points (E). We used 10-point Palatino for the body text, increased the initial cap to 24 points, and specified an overall leading of 12.5 points.

W hen action grows unprofitable, gather information; when information grows unprofitable, sleep.
— *Ursula K. Le Guin*

Defining a drop cap

A *drop cap* is taller than the body text, with its top or "ascent" aligned to the ascent of the first line of text. The drop cap is called "2-line," "3-line," and so on, depending on how far into the text its baseline extends. Shown here is a 2-line drop cap. A drop cap can be created by using the Drop Cap Addition or by setting the letter as a text block separate from the body text.

A When action grows un-profitable, gather informa-tion; when information grows unprofitable, sleep. — *Ursula K. Le Guin*

B
| Drop cap | OK |
| Wrap 2 lines | Cancel |

C 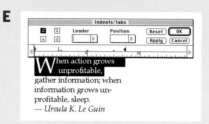 When action grows unprofitable, gather information; when information grows un-profitable, sleep. — *Ursula K. Le Guin*

D When action grows unprofitable, gather information; when information grows un-profitable, sleep. — *Ursula K. Le Guin*

E 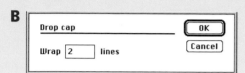 When action grows unprofitable, gather information; when information grows un-profitable, sleep. — *Ursula K. Le Guin*

F 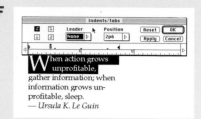 When action grows unprofitable, gather information; when information grows un-profitable, sleep. — *Ursula K. Le Guin*

G When action grows unprofitable, gather information; when infor-mation grows unprofit-able, sleep. — *Ursula K. Le Guin*

Using the Drop Cap Addition

To use the Drop Cap Addition, choose it from the Aldus Additions submenu under the Utilities menu after you have selected a paragraph (A), and specify the number of text lines to wrap around the capital. For this example, set in 11/13-point Palatino, we chose 2 (B). The Drop Caps command automatically enlarges the initial letter of the paragraph, converts it to a subscript character, shifts the baseline of the subscript down, inserts tabs to move the text to the right of the initial cap, and enters line breaks at the ends of the lines that wrap around the initial cap (C). In our example, when the second letter of the paragraph and the first letter of the second line did not line up (D), we selected the first two lines and chose Indents/Tabs from the Type menu (E), then moved the first tab to the left so it lined up with the second letter of the paragraph (F). This moved the start of the second line to the proper position (G). ● *To create a drop cap of a different font than the rest of the paragraph, select the letter and change its font before using Drop Caps.*

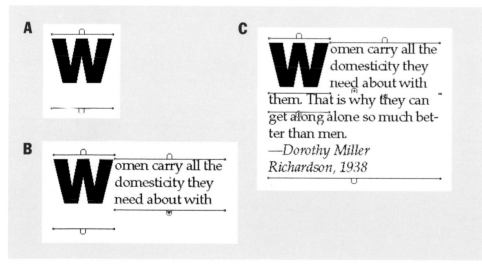

A W

B W omen carry all the domesticity they need about with

C W omen carry all the domesticity they need about with them. That is why they can get along alone so much bet-ter than men. —*Dorothy Miller Richardson, 1938*

A Aesthetic emotion puts man in a state favorable to the reception of erotic emotion. Art is the accom-plice of love. Take love away and there is no longer art. — *Remy de Gourmont, 1858–1915*

B A esthetic emotion puts man in a state favorable to the reception of erotic emotion. Art is the accom-plice of love. Take love away and there is no longer art. — *Remy de Gourmont, 1858–1915*

C A esthetic emotion puts man in a state favorable to the recep-tion of erotic emotion. Art is the accomplice of love. Take love away and there is no longer art. — *Remy de Gourmont, 1858–1915*

Creating separate drop caps

We started by typing the initial cap as a separate text block (A). We positioned the text block for the rest of the paragraph next to the cap, dragged its lower handle so that 3 lines were visible, and changed the size of the cap until it matched the height of the 3 lines. The red arrow indicated that there was more text (B). We clicked on the arrow to get the rest of the text and positioned this block below the drop cap, aligning the top of this text block to the bottom of the top block (C).

Creating a hanging raised cap

A *hanging cap* is one that is positioned to the left of the body text with no text wrapped beneath it. A *raised hanging cap*, shown here, has the same baseline as the first line of text. We set our ex-ample in 10-point Berkeley Medium with 12-point leading (A) and increased the point size of the first letter to 30 (B). We then used the margin and paragraph settings in the Indents/Tabs dialog box to indent the subsequent lines to match the position of the second letter of the paragraph (C).

A

No house should ever be *on* any hill or on anything. It should be *of* the hill, belonging to it, so hill and house could live together each the happier for the other.
— *Frank Lloyd Wright, 1932*

B

N o house should *ever* be *on* any hill or on anything. It should be *of* the hill, belonging to it, so hill and house could live together each the happier for the other.
— *Frank Lloyd Wright, 1932*

C

N o house should ever be *on* any hill or on anything. It should be *of* the hill, belonging to it, so hill and house could live together each the happier for the other.
— *Frank Lloyd Wright, 1932*

Creating a hanging drop cap

A *hanging drop cap* has its top aligned with the top of the body text and its baseline aligned with the second or a subsequent line. To create a 2-line hanging drop cap we set a paragraph in 10-point Berkeley (A) and then selected the first letter, cut it, pasted it into a separate text block, increased its size to 30 points (B), and positioned it to the left of the paragraph text block (C).

Importing initial caps

Decorative letters can be scanned from books of copyright-free art, saved in TIFF format, and imported into PageMaker with the Place command. The 2 "B's" shown here are Victorian initials, and the "T" is an Art Nouveau initial. All were scanned at 266 dpi. Decorative letters in PostScript format are also available.

A

To live content with small means; to seek elegance rather than luxury, and refinement rather than fashion; to be worthy, not respectable, and wealthy, not rich; to study hard, think quietly, talk gently, act frankly; to listen to stars and birds, to babes and sages, with open heart; to bear all cheerfully, do all bravely, await occasions, hurry never. In a word, to let the spiritual, unbidden and unconscious, grow up through the common. This is to be my symphony.
— *William Henry Channing, 1810–1884*

B

T o live content with small means; to seek elegance rather than luxury, and refinement rather than fashion; to be worthy, not respectable, and wealthy, not rich; to study hard, think quietly, talk gently, act frankly; to listen to stars and birds, to babes and sages, with open heart; to bear all cheerfully, do all bravely, await occasions, hurry never. In a word, to let the spiritual, unbidden and unconscious, grow up through the common. This is to be my symphony.
— *William Henry Channing, 1810–1884*

C

T o live content with small means; to seek elegance rather than luxury, and refinement rather than fashion; to be worthy, not respectable, and wealthy, not rich; to study hard, think quietly, talk gently, act frankly; to listen to stars and birds, to babes and sages, with open heart; to bear all cheerfully, do all bravely, await occasions, hurry never. In a word, to let the spiritual, unbidden and unconscious, grow up through the common. This is to be my symphony.
— *William Henry Channing, 1810–1884*

Wrapping type around an imported cap

Because an imported initial functions as a graphic, it can easily be used to create a drop cap. Use the Text Wrap dialog box from the Element menu to make it repellent so that adjacent body text wraps around it. To create this example, we set a paragraph in 10-point Berkeley Medium (A), then selected and deleted the first letter, imported an initial cap in TIFF format, and positioned it over the upper left corner of the text block. We dragged the lower right corner handle of the graphic with the Shift key held down until the height of the letter matched the first 5 lines of text (B), and then used the Text Wrap dialog box to specify that the text flow around the graphic with a stand-off of about 4 points (C).

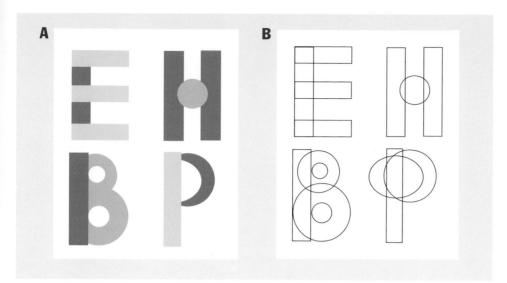

Drawing initial caps

Just as the ellipse, rectangle, and line tools can be used to create illustrations, these drawing tools can also be used to create custom initial caps (A). A keyline view shows how the letters were constructed (B). The curved part of the "P" was created by covering part of a blue circle with a white ellipse. The left edge of the ellipse is invisible against the white background.

Combining type with shapes

Original initial caps can be created by combining shapes drawn with the drawing tools with type from various fonts. To create a decorative "S," we combined a character in Helvetica Light with 2 circles. To make a special "F," we combined 2 Zapf Dingbats arrows with a vertical rectangle. To create a decorative "O" we placed a Zapf Dingbats heart character inside a circle.

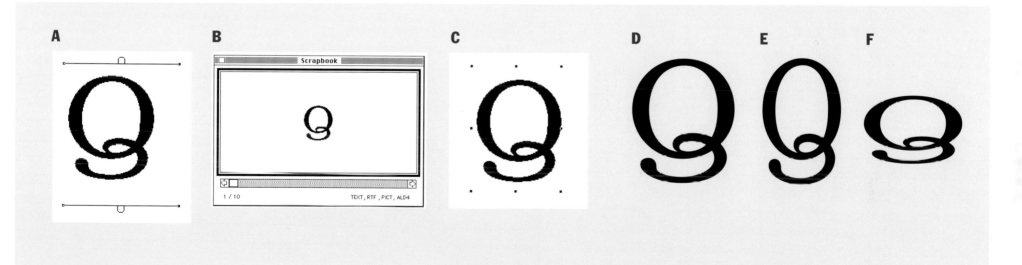

Using Scrapbook type

It is possible to convert type into a graphic element that can then be distorted or made to repel other type. We first typed a "Q" in Bookman, which is shown here in its text block (A). We selected the "Q" with the pointer tool (not the text tool), chose Copy from the Edit menu, then chose Scrapbook from the apple menu. We chose Paste to put the "Q" into the Scrapbook (B), then chose Place from the File menu and double-clicked on the Scrapbook file in the System folder to bring the "Q," now a graphic element, into PageMaker (C). Once the "Q" was a graphic element, it could be scaled proportionately by dragging any corner handle with the Shift key held down (D) or scaled vertically (E) or horizontally (F) by dragging without the Shift key. ⌘ *The last element put into the Scrapbook is the first out when the Scrapbook icon is clicked in PageMaker.*

A

M usic I heard with you was more than music, and bread I broke with you was more than bread.
— Conrad Aiken, 1914

B

M usic I heard with you was more than music, and bread I broke with you was more than bread.
— Conrad Aiken, 1914

C

M usic I heard with you was more than music, and bread I broke with you was more than bread.
— Conrad Aiken, 1914

Creating boxed caps

You can imitate the look of a custom initial cap by placing a letter typed in PageMaker inside a box drawn with the rectangle tool. The rest of the text can then be wrapped around the box, which functions as a graphic element. We created several variations, including a black letter in a white box (A), a reversed letter in a black box (B), and a letter and box in 2 colors (C). The type used for the initial caps was Berkeley, FreeStyle Script, and Brush Script for A, B, and C respectively. ⬤ *To prevent the letter itself from being repelled by the text wrap specifications of the box, specify a negative leading for the letter, at about half its point size.*

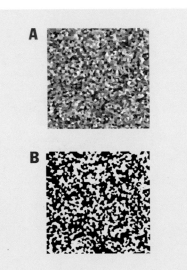

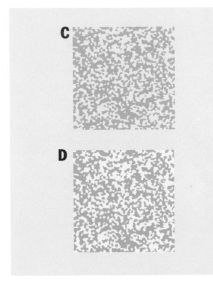

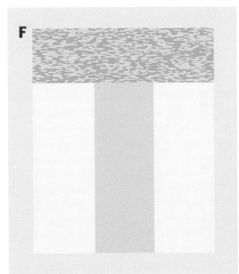

Creating a cap on a textured background

To make a 2-color textured background for an initial capital, we first created a randomized texture in Adobe Photoshop by using the Add Noise and Crystallize filters (A). Then we converted it from color to black-and-white (A).

and saved it as a TIFF (B). We placed the TIFF in PageMaker and gave it a color by clicking on a color name in the Colors palette (C). Then we drew a rectangle, filled it with a contrasting color, and used Send To Back to position it behind the TIFF (D). To complete

the initial cap, we typed a letter in Frutiger Ultra Black, colored it a darker shade than the background colors, and positioned it over the textured rectangle (E). We used the same TIFF to make the crossbar of a custom letter "T." First we dragged the TIFF's handles to create a

horizontal rectangle. The rectangle tool was used to add the "T's" upright and a background shape, in 2 additional colors (F).

17

Using
Initial Caps: 1

John Odam

Designers sometimes use very large or dramatic initial caps to create strong graphic elements for a page, especially when other illustration possibilities are limited.

Using initial caps as design elements

Verbum is a magazine devoted to computer art and culture. To emphasize the versatility of desktop publishing, art director John Odam creates a different page design for each issue. For this article spread he made bold use of an initial cap as a structural element. "Type is the cheapest way to illustrate a page," says Odam. The oversize cap, set in Gill Sans Ultra Bold was colored 40% gray and placed partially behind the text.

Varying the initial cap treatment

Odam used initial caps in Gill Sans throughout the issue in varying positions to lend drama and unity to the pages. In this opening page for the *Verbum* interview, the cap is positioned in the upper left of the page, and the first column of text, set in Goudy, runs over it.

Using 3D caps

For another issue of *Verbum* Odam set the article title in a 3D face called Umbra and then used a 300-point version colored gray as an initial cap. At this large size the cap almost becomes an abstract shape. The body text was set in Utopia.

Creating a reversed cap

For the opening page of a *Verbum* article that features dramatic black-and-white graphics, Odam created a complementary initial cap by placing a large reversed "R" set in Avant Garde over a black rectangle. The body text was set in Palatino.

Combining two fonts

For a *Verbum* issue devoted to "blendo," or the convergence of cultures and art forms, Odam echoed the theme by placing a curving gray script "a" set in Linotext over a heavy black "A" set in Helvetica Black.

18

Using Initial Caps: 2

Diane Fenster

Sometimes, in order to be able to use special effects that are impossible to achieve in PageMaker, designers create initial caps in other programs and import them into page layouts.

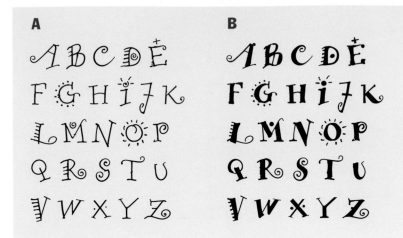

1 Starting with a decorative font

To create an initial cap treatment for the opening pages of articles in a science magazine, designer Diane Fenster started with decorative fonts called Remedy Single (A) and Remedy Double (B) from Emigre Graphics. The fanciful letters provide a contrast for the scientific writing in the magazine, *Intersci,* published by the School of Science at San Francisco State University.

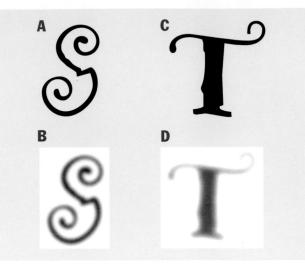

2 Applying a blur effect

Fenster planned to combine initial caps created in PageMaker with blurred versions created in Adobe Photoshop. She first opened Photoshop, typed an "S" in Remedy Single (A) and applied the Gaussian Blur filter (B) to produce the initial cap she needed for an article. She typed a "T" in Remedy Double (C) and applied the same filter to create an initial cap for a pull quote (D).

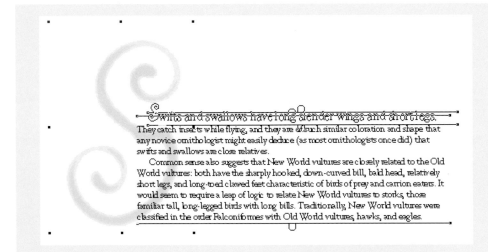

3 Combining large and small caps

For the opening paragraph of the article Fenster set the body type in 11/13-point Goudy and emphasized the first line by setting it in 15/15-point Fenice. She set the first letter in 30-point Remedy Single and then imported the blurred "S," enlarged it in PageMaker, and placed it behind and to the left of the paragraph. To make it easier to read the body text over the blurred initial cap, she applied a tint of 25% black by clicking on this color in the Color palette while the "S" was selected.

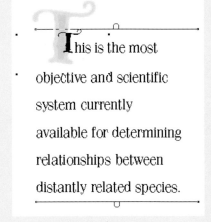

4 Using a variation for pull quotes

Fenster set a pull quote in 17/30-point Fenice, set the initial "T" in 35-point Remedy Double, and then imported the blurred "T" and applied a 25% tint of black. The finished page includes a clip art graphic, a decorative department head, and 2 columns of body type.

19

Creating Custom Column Shapes

PageMaker's column guides form text into rectangular blocks. But you can create text blocks in diagonal or curved shapes by using the Text Wrap functions.

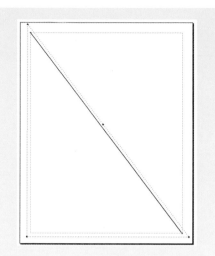

1 Creating a triangular column shape

To create a text block with a diagonal edge, we first drew a 0.5-point diagonal line, chose Text Wrap from the Element menu, and clicked on the center icon under Wrap Option. This drew a rectangular text wrap boundary around the diagonal line.

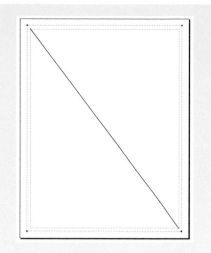

2 Editing the text wrap boundary

To make the text wrap boundary into a triangle shape that would repel type, we dragged its upper right corner handle down toward the diagonal line, dragged the upper left handle up slightly, and dragged the lower right handle a little to the right.

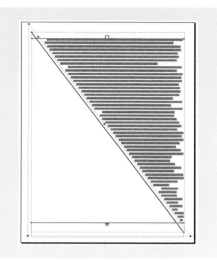

3 Positioning the text

We set a block of type and positioned it on the page in a single wide column. The text wrap boundary associated with the diagonal line repelled the type so that it was forced into a triangular shape.

4 Making the repelling object invisible

Once the text block and text wrap boundary were as we wanted, we selected the diagonal line and changed its Element, Line specification to None so that it would not be visible when the page was printed.

5 Adding a headline

We added a headline in 72-point Franklin Gothic Demi. To keep the headline from also being repelled we placed it entirely within the text wrap boundary.

6 Completing the page

We finished the design by adding an initial capital, a background color and simple graphic, and 8-point black rules that tie the headline to the text column.

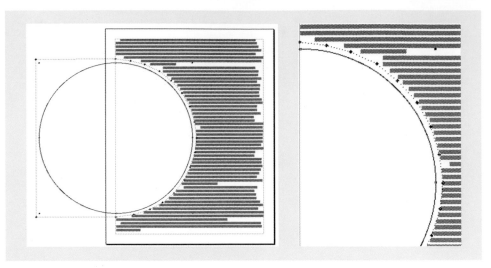

7 Creating a curved column shape

To create a curved column shape we drew a 0.5-point circle and applied text wrap, which created a square boundary around the circle. We then adjusted the text wrap boundary to follow the curve along the right side of the circle. To do this we clicked on the circle's boundary at even intervals to add new handles and moved the handles close to the edge of the circle. ● *To keep text from re-wrapping each time you move a handle, hold down the space bar until you finish adjusting.*

8 Making the text wrap boundary invisible

As with the previous example, we changed the specification of the circle from a 0.5-point black line to None so that it would not show on screen or when the page was printed.

9 Finishing the design

We finished the page by adding a headline in 72-point ITC Century Ultra Condensed and a 20% gray background rectangle that links the headline to the text.

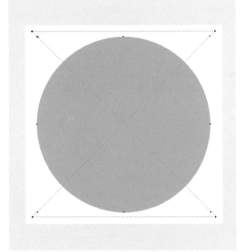

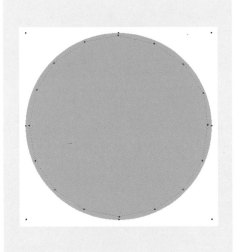

10 Putting text into a circle

Text can be wrapped *inside* a circle shape by turning its text wrap boundaries "inside out." The first step is to draw a circle and apply a standard text wrap specification, which produces a square boundary.

11 Reversing the text wrap boundary

To reverse the boundary we first dragged the upper right handle to the left and the upper left handle to the right. Notice that the boundary outline criss-crosses over itself.

12 Completing the reversal

Next we dragged the lower right handle of the boundary to the left and dragged the lower left handle to the right. The boundary now looks "normal" again, but will wrap text differently because it has been reversed.

13 Fitting the boundary to the circle

We clicked along the edges of the boundary to create new handles and dragged them inward so that there were 16 handles evenly spaced along the inside edge of the circle.

52 ALDUS PAGEMAKER: A VISUAL GUIDE FOR THE MAC

A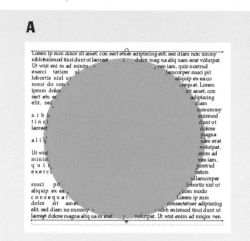

B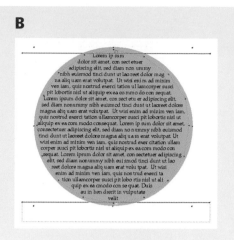

C

15 Using inner and outer boundaries

14 Placing the text over the circle

We set a block of type in Palatino and placed it over the circle. If the text block is positioned with all of its edges outside the boundary, the text is wrapped outside (A). We positioned the text block so its upper edge was below the circle's text wrap boundary and its lower and side edges were outside. So long as the text is positioned with one edge inside, the boundary wraps the text inside of the circle (B). Type size and line breaks can be adjusted to make the text fit the way you want. The finished PageMaker version is shown here (C).

15 Using inner and outer boundaries

We wrapped our text into a doughnut shape by placing a smaller tan circle with a standard text wrap in the center of the blue circle with the "inside out" text wrap.

A **B** **C**
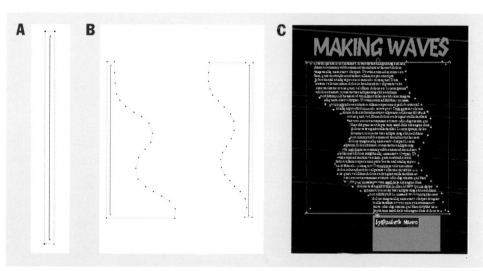

16 Adjusting text wrap boundaries

The text wrap boundary around an object can be edited to any shape by simply adding or deleting handles and dragging them to the desired position. ● *To delete a handle, drag it over a neighboring handle.*

17 Creating a graphic text block shape

Text blocks can be shaped into any contours by creating custom text wrap boundaries around objects with a Fill and Line of None. We used this technique to flow a text block into a triangle shape.

18 Using 2 text wrap boundaries

We used 2 text wrap boundaries to force a column of text into a wave shape. We drew a straight line and applied a text wrap (A), added and moved handles from the right-hand boundary edge to create a wave shape, and created another line with a wave boundary along its left edge (B). We placed a block of Palatino text across both boundary objects (C) and added color and headline type in Emigre's Elektrix Bold to complete the design. The finished design is shown on page 5.

20

Varying Styles for Nameplates and Titles

PageMaker's type functions make it possible to create and edit type to produce designs for nameplates, letterhead designs, and other short titles in a variety of styles.

Janet Ashford

A CITYLIFE

B CITY*life*

C CITY*Life*

Contrasting serif with sans serif fonts
Starting with a simple nameplate set in Times (A), we changed the type to Optima and Snell Roundhand to contrast the words "city" and "life" (B). Another variation features Frutiger Black and Mistral, whose irregularities add an appropriate liveliness to the word (C).

A **Thick** &Thin

B **DIETING** NEWS

Contrasting heavy with light weights
We set "thick" in Garamond Ultra with a Set Width of 80% and "thin" in Garamond Light Condensed to provide a graphic contrast to back up the meaning of the words (A). We used 5 different weights of Frutiger for a news-letter on weight loss and applied a Set Width of 60% to both words (B).

BANKING
NOTES

Contrasting point sizes
When 1 word of a publication's title is more important than the other, this can be emphasized with a larger point size. We used a 72-point size for "Banking" and a 24-point size for "Notes," both in Garamond Book Condensed.

Old Time Music
Herald

Old Time Music
Herald

Embedding 1 type block into another
When the last word of a title includes interior letters with no ascenders (letters like "a" and "e "as opposed to "d" and "k"), you can take advantage of the space to hold the first word or words of the title, set in a smaller size. We used Century Light Condensed for this example and added some rectangle frames.

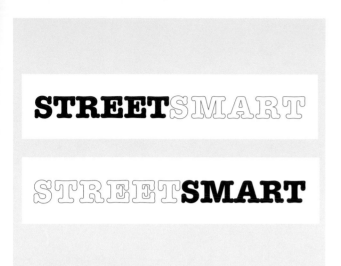

Contrasting type styles

We set "Streetsmart" in American Typewriter bold, then styled the last 5 letters in Outline mode. Reversing the normal and outline styles also works well to distinguish the 2 parts of this compound word.

Contrasting black and white or colors

Placing reversed type over a black background and black type over white provides interest for a nameplate. We used Garamond Book Condensed for our example. A pair of contrasting colors can also be used.

Creating drop shadows

A 3-dimensional effect can be created by making a copy of a text block, changing its color, and offsetting the copy over the original. The drop shadow effect varies depending on how much and in what direction the copy is moved in relation to the original.

Using horizontal lines with type

Horizontal rules can be used to unify the characters of a title, provide decoration, and reinforce meaning. We used Bodoni Poster Compressed over 0.5-point blue lines for a writer's newsletter. For a bus pamphlet we used 1-point white lines over red type in Futura Bold Oblique to emphasize motion.

Using geometric elements

Circles, ellipses, and rectangles can be added to type to create special effects. For "On Target" we placed a bold red circle behind an uppercase "O" set in Bodoni Bold, and set the rest of the nameplate in Bodoni Poster Compressed. For "Directions" we typed a 72-point Zapf Dingbats triangle, rotated it 90 de-

grees, changed its color to yellow, and positioned it over a black rectangle along with 2 copies. Reverse type set in Brush Script completed the design.

A
BULLETIN

B
BULLETIN

C
BULLETIN

D
B U L L E T I N

E
• BUSINESS •
B U L L E T I N

A
B U L L E T I N

B
B•U•L•L•E•T•I•N

C
B•U•L•L•E•T•I•N

Using letterspacing for effect

Adding extra space between letters creates an elegant look and works especially well with condensed typefaces like Futura Condensed. We started with text set with Normal track (A). You can add space by applying a Very Loose track (B), by pressing the space bar between letters (C), or by specifying Force Justify and pulling the handles on the right side of the text block to the right (D). We added background rectangles and more text to create a finished nameplate (E).

Adding and adjusting bullets

You can add bullets in the spaces between letters for a decorative effect. Begin by typing Option-8 between letters (A). Then make the bullets smaller by specifying them as Superscripts in the Type Specs dialog box (B). Adjust the Superscript position until the bullets are centered vertically (C).

A
BULLETIN

B
B♥ULLETIN

C
B♥ULLETIN

D
B♥ULLETIN

E
B♥ULLETIN

F
B•U•L•L•E•T•I•N

G
Valentine
B♥U♥L♥L♥E♥T♥I♥N

Using dingbats as bullets

To use a dingbat as a bullet, type a title (we used Garamond Book Condensed) (A), insert a dingbat between the first 2 letters (B), and convert it to a Superscript (C). Open the Type Options dialog box (by clicking Options in the Type Specs dialog box) and decrease the Super/subscript size to 40% (D). Decrease the amount in the Superscript position field so that the dingbat is centered vertically (E). Copy the dingbat and paste it between the other pairs of letters, change the Track to Very Loose (F), and then add decorative elements (G). Changing the point size will change the superscripts proportionately, keeping the nameplate design intact as it gets larger or smaller.

Using kerning with baseline shifts

A line of type can be recessed into the interior space of a large initial cap to create a nameplate. We started by typing a title in 18-point Gill Sans (A) and then selected and enlarged the initial cap to 60 points (B). We selected the small type, chose Type Specs from the Type menu, and clicked on Options.

We entered a value of 17 points and clicked the "up" button for Baseline Shift to raise the small type from the bottom of the "C" to its center (C). We then inserted the text cursor between the "C" and the "e" and typed Option-Delete several times to kern the "e" to the left (D). We added colored background shapes to complete the design (E).

Drawing custom letters

We used circles, rectangles, a diagonal line, and type set in Franklin Gothic to create a colorful, custom nameplate. The design is shown with black lines and no fill (A) and with solid colored fills (B).

Rotating text

Type can be rotated in 0.01-degree increments using either the rotating tool in the toolbox or the Rotating option in the Control palette. We set type for a nameplate in Frutiger Ultra Black in 2 separate text blocks (A) and used the rotating tool to rotate the word "the" by +90 degrees. We positioned the 2 text blocks and added color and a background to complete the design. ⬤ *To constrain rotation to 45-degree increments from the starting position, hold down the Shift key as you rotate an object with the rotating tool.*

Using pattern backgrounds

We imported a black-and-white pattern that had been saved as a bitmap so that its white areas were transparent (A). We colored the bitmap gray and placed it over a pale blue background, which shows through the transparent areas. Type in Garamond Book italic was placed on top (B).

Creating a
Nameplate: 1

RAINBOW
CONNECTION

A PUBLICATION OF THE ALTERNATIVE PROGRAM
SKYLINE SCHOOL, SOLANA BEACH, CALIFORNIA

SCHOOL NEWS

Social Studies

We are now ready to begin our study of the native peoples of North America. For this unit we begin with a review of the idea that we all migrated here but there were people already here that migrated to North America *much* earlier. Throughout this unit we must confront the stereotyping of Indians as all on horses with tepees. We also need to increase students' awareness of the contributions that Native Americans make to our country today. This study will culminate with a cross age study unit where each child is assigned to a "tribe." Kids from Bobbie's class will be acting as docents for the study of the tribes. Each group will be responsible for cooking a simulated typical food,

building a model of a traditional home, decorating a field-sized paper doll, developing "costumes" for the Pow Wow Day and placing that culture within a geographical and environmental context. You are welcome to attend that day. In fact, we will need additional volunteer to work with the tribes. Let us know if you can help. Also, if you have any materials to help us address these areas. We especially need items noting the life of these tribes today and Native American role models, biographies, etc. Our author of the month will be, Native American Legends. Please label items you bring in. Thanks.

Continued on page 4

Calendar

Oct. 2, Wednesday, Parent Meeting, Open Agenda, 3:30 PM

Oct. 31, Thursday, Halloween class party and costume parade

Nov. 6, Wednesday, Parent meeting

Nov. 8, Friday, Tentative Pow Wow Day (may have to be moved to the 16th; we will notify you soon)

Sharing Topics

Week of Oct 7–11, Picture and story from newspaper; be able to tell who, what, where?

Oct 21–25, A memorized Halloween poem

Oct 28–Nov 1, Open

Nov 4–8, Piece of clothing from a country other than U.S.

• OCTOBER •

Janet Ashford

The nameplate of a newsletter or magazine includes the name of the publication and often integrates the issue date or a subheading. Nameplates in a variety of styles can be created in PageMaker.

RAINBOW
CONNECTION

1 Choosing a typeface

To create a nameplate for an elementary school newsletter, we began by typing the title in all caps and specifying the font as Franklin Gothic Heavy. We selected the type and tried several different point sizes until we found a size, 61 points, that made the longer word, "Connection," fit the 2-column-wide space (5.625 inches) designated for the nameplate.

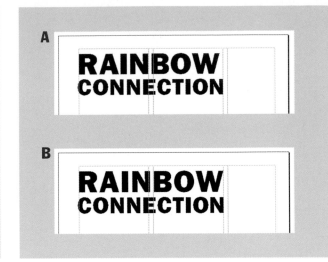

2 Adjusting point sizes and letter spacing

By trial and error we increased the point size of the shorter word, "Rainbow," to 81 points, so that it almost filled the available space (A). Then we inserted the cursor into each of the spaces between letters in both words and typed Option-Shift-Delete to increase the width of the letterspace by 0.01 em each time. This process was repeated until each word exactly filled the space (B).

RAINBOW
CONNECTION

3 Adding horizontal rules

To unify the 2 lines of type, we used the line tool to draw a 12-point horizontal line the width of the type, then copied the line twice and positioned the lines above, below, and between the 2 lines of type.

RAINBOW
CONNECTION

A PUBLICATION OF THE ALTERNATIVE PROGRAM
SKYLINE SCHOOL, SOLANA BEACH, CALIFORNIA

4 Adding a subhead and placing the nameplate

A subhead identifying the school was set in 11-point Franklin Gothic Roman. The nameplate was positioned in the upper left corner of the cover (as shown at the left) and its bottom rule was extended to span the width of the text area. The silhouette graphic echoes the heavy use of black in the nameplate.

22
Creating a Nameplate: 2

For a newsletter, designer John Odam dealt with a long title by creating a nameplate in which the title is set in relatively small type and integrated with a large, decorative logo.

California Indian Energy News is a publication of the California Energy Extension Service, an Energy Management Action Program of the Office of Governor Pete Wilson

1 Setting and kerning the type
Odam began by typing the title in ITC Century Italic, in reversed type on a black background. To distinguish the group (California Indians) from the topic (Energy News), he used bold for the first 2 words and light for the second 2 (A). To refine the type's letterspacing, he selected it and applied a Tight Track (B), and then used Option-Shift-Delete keystrokes to separate the letters slightly by inserting letterspace in increments of 0.01 em to get exactly the spacing he wanted (C).

3 Adding a subhead
To the left of the nameplate Odam added a small block of type set in Century that identifies the issue date, the organization, and its logo. He extended the thin rule under the title bar to link it with the subhead. The nameplate and subhead were placed at the top of the cover page, which also includes a photo that bleeds off the bottom and type in Century and Franklin Gothic.

2 Completing the type unit
Odam created a black rectangle to fit the space available on the newsletter cover (it spanned 4 columns of a 5-column grid), allowed for an amount to bleed off the top of the page, and added a hairline accent rule under the rectangle (A). He then imported a sun graphic created in Aldus FreeHand. He positioned it below the type and rectangle and sized it to the same width (B).

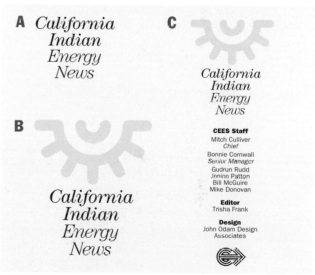

4 Creating a variation for the masthead
To create a thinner version of the nameplate for the masthead, Odam typed the title in 4 lines, applied a Tight track, then used kerning keystrokes to spread the type slightly (A). He placed a scaled copy of the sun graphic above the type (B) and placed both above the single-column masthead listings (C).

23

Creating a Nameplate: 3

John Odam

A nameplate constructed only of type can serve as a primary graphic element for a publication, as for this folk music newsletter.

A
B

1 Setting and sizing type

For the nameplate of the *Folk Notes* folk music newsletter, John Odam set 180-point Aachen type with Normal track (A). He selected the 3 interior letters and changed the point size to 126 points and the track to Loose (B).

A
B

2 Adjusting horizontal width

To make the letters thinner, Odam used the Set Width command to decrease the horizontal scale of the letters from 100% (A) to 67% (B). The height of the letters was not affected.

A
B

3 Kerning and adding a box

To fill the 5.375-inch space available for the nameplate, Odam used the Option-Shift-Delete command to add space between the letters (A). With the rectangle tool he drew a horizontal box above the inner letters (B).

A
B

4 Adding reverse type

Odam used the black rectangle as a frame for the first word of the nameplate, which he set in 56-point New Baskerville italic, in white (A). He kerned the letters (Option-Shift-Delete) to spread them apart (B).

5 Adding ornaments

Odam added a white ornament on either side of the word "Folk" by copying a single character from the Woodtype Ornaments font. One of the copies was reflected using the Horizontal-reflecting button on the Control palette. The finished nameplate was placed in the upper right corner of the cover page, where it provides an eye-catching balance for the type on the rest of the page.

24
Using Vertical Headlines

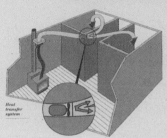

Large headlines rotated to a vertical orientation can make a bold graphic statement on a page, especially when used as a complement to existing elements such as initial caps, subheads, and borders.

1 Setting the type
For *California Indian Energy News*, designer John Odam created a vertical headline for an article about wood. He first set the type Century Light italic using 120 points for the first letter and 140 points in Small Caps for the rest (the type is shown smaller here). He used Normal track and assigned a 30% black color (A). He then placed the text cursor between the 2 "O's" and typed Command-Delete 8 times to delete 0.04 em at each stroke until the "O's" were overlapped (B).

2 Rotating the headline
Odam selected the headline with the pointer tool (not the text tool) and then used the Control palette to rotate the text block +90 degrees. ◆ *Positive numbers rotate objects counterclockwise while negative numbers rotate objects clockwise.*

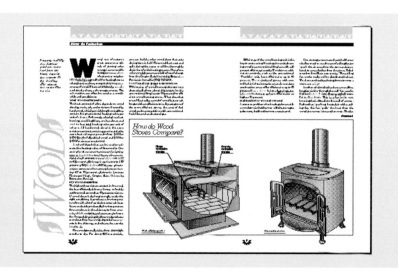

3 Placing the headline in the layout
Odam placed the headline along the bottom left edge of the article's opening spread and added 2 flame symbols imported from Aldus FreeHand. He repeated the headline on the next page (see opening art) in order to tie the 3 pages together. The curving lines of the type, its vertical orientation, and its gray color contrast well with the heavy black initial cap and horizontal borders on the page.

California Indian Energy News is a publication of the California Energy Extension Service, an Energy Management Action Program of the Office of Governor Pete Wilson.

Creating Department Heads: 1

Janet Ashford

HEALTHWATCH

SIDS and Sleeping Prone

Drawing from a compilation of studies done on an international scale, researchers are now concluding that infants in the first six months of life are at increased risk of Sudden Infant Death Syndrome if they are placed in the prone position (on their stomachs) to sleep. Reports from the Netherlands, Great Britain, Australia, and New Zealand indicated that avoiding the prone position could reduce the number of SIDS deaths up to 50 percent.

An exceptionally low rate of SIDS in Hong Kong and the South Sea Islands has been attributed to a cultural preference there for the supine position (on the back) for sleeping infants, and a high rate of SIDS among the Maoris has been attributed to their favoring the prone. In 1972, a public campaign in the Netherlands discouraged parents from placing their infants in the supine sleeping position; before that year the Netherlands' incidence of SIDS had been one of the lowest in the Western world (.46 per 1000 live births). Following the public campaign, the SIDS rate rose to 1.31 per 1000.
(*Journal of the American Medical Association*, May 6, 1992. As reported in *Midwifery Today*, Summer 1992.)

Baby-Friendly Hospital Initiative

The World Alliance for Breastfeeding Action and UNICEF have made an evaluation form available that can be completed by new mothers and shared with hospital administrators and health workers. The Baby-Friendly Hospital Initiative Survey enables new mothers to evaluate how well a hospital promotes breastfeeding. The goal is to help improve hospital services. To supply your practice with copies of the Initiative, write to UNICEF House, 3 United Nations Plaza, New York, NY 10017, or use the Baby-Friendly Hospital Initiative Fax Hotline, 212-303-7911.

Newborn Bill of Rights

The newborn has the right to:

1. Be born in as natural, loving and family-centered setting as possible with a knowledgeable, caring, conscientious birth attendant, either at home, in a birth center, or a progressive, family-centered hospital, as best meets the particular needs of the family.

2. Be born vaginally, without intervention, drugs, induced labor, forceps, electronic fetal monitor, artificial rupture of the membranes, or any other aggressive obstetrical procedure, barring absolute health necessity.

3. Be born in the presence of his/her father and be held immediately after birth by the mother and father, barring absolute health contraindications. (Some hospitals allow the mother to hold her baby five minutes or so on the delivery table before taking him or her away. This does not constitute uninterrupted bonding.)

4. Be kept warm after birth. Dangerous consequences can result from the loss of body heat. In most cases, the mother's body insures adequate warmth if the baby is covered with a blanket.

5. Be fed on demand, in accordance with his/her body's need for food, rather than by an arbitrary imposed schedule. All babies should be considered for breastfeeding, as breastmilk has been proven to be the superior food for infants.

6. Be spared any painful procedure that is not absolutely necessary for his/her health or well being, such as the routine administration of silver nitrate drops in the eyes. This procedure is useless for the 95% of all babies whose mothers do not have gonorrhea. Prophylactic ointments such as erythromycin or tetracy-

cline, which do not sting, can be used.

7. Be afforded necessary and appropriate treatment in the event of abnormality or illness, with all decisions being made with only the welfare of the child in mind. If a procedure is necessary, such as surgery for a hernia or other birth defect, the infant has the right to have appropriate, effective anaesthesia, since all older individuals undergoing surgery are afforded this consideration.

8. Be allowed to keep all normally occurring parts of his/her body, including the foreskin, which is a useful, protective piece of body tissue.

9. Be spared any cosmetic procedure that involves body alteration of normal structures, until the child is old enough to choose for him/herself whether or not he/she wishes it. Therefore, tattooing of a child's body, piercing of a child's ears or circumcising a child's foreskin, done merely for the sake of the parent's sense of aesthetics, is a basic violation of individual human rights, because the child cannot make a choice about it.

10. Be spared procedures done for demonstration and/or teaching purposes and routine procedures that exist only for the few who may need it.

For more information contact:
NEWBORN RIGHTS SOCIETY
P.O. Box 48
St. Peters, Pennsylvania, USA 19407-0048
(From *The Compleat Mother*, Fall 1992)

California Association of Midwives • Winter 1992–93 • 1

Placing reverse type on black rectangle backgrounds is an easy way to create effective department headings for a newsletter.

A — In the Courts

B — IN THE COURTS

C —
IN THE COURTS
LEGISLATIVE NEWS
REGIONAL REPORTS
NEWS & NOTICES

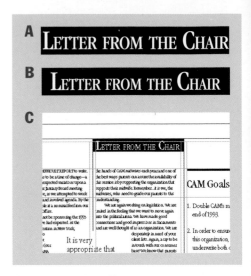

A — LETTER FROM THE CHAIR

B — LETTER FROM THE CHAIR

C —

1 Setting, styling, and reversing the type

To create simple department heads for the California Association of Midwives newsletter, the type was set in 28-point Garamond Book Condensed (A). The type was selected and small caps and a Loose track were specified (B). Each line of department head type was reversed and placed in the center of a black rectangle that filled the 2.5-inch single-column width (shown smaller here) of the 3-column newsletter. The length of most of the headings fit well inside the rectangles (C).

2 Adjusting a long line

One of the department head titles was too long to fit comfortably in the rectangle (A), so the size of the small letters was reduced to 25 points (B), to make the title the same width as the text column (C).

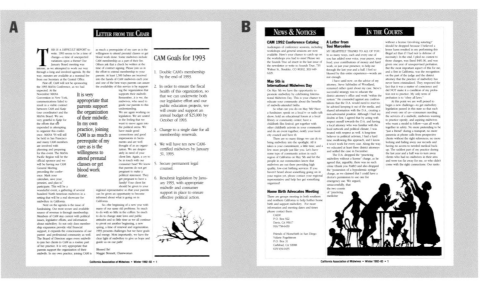

3 Placing the heads in the layout

In cases where a single department took up an entire page, the department head was placed at the top of the center column. The columns are marked off by vertical rules, and the department head fits snugly between the rules (A). In cases where more than 1 department appeared on a page, the department head was placed at the top of a left or right column, or in the center of a 2-column spread (B). The use of black silhouette graphics balances the black of the department heads.

26

Creating Department Heads: 2

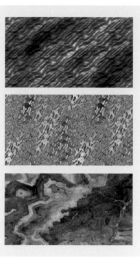

Scanned textures drawn from scientific subjects make handsome backgrounds for reversed department heads.

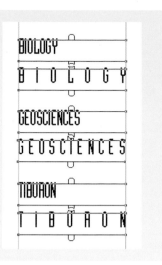

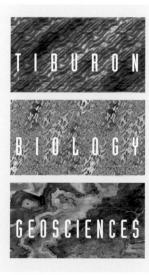

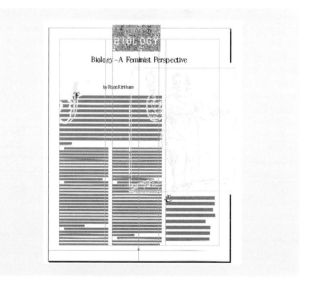

1 Creating a textured department head

To create department heads for *InterSci*, a publication of the San Francisco State University School of Science, designer Diane Fenster scanned photographs of various scientific images and used Adobe Photoshop to crop them each to the same 1.25 x 2 .25-inch size and to save them as grayscale TIFFs.

2 Setting the type

Fenster set type for each of the department heads in 30-point Industria Solid, then dragged the text block to fit the width of the textured backgrounds and specified Force Justify, which spread the characters to fill the text block.

3 Reversing the type over the background

Fenster imported the texture TIFFs into PageMaker and positioned them on the appropriate pages. She then specified reverse type for each of the heads and placed the type for each over the appropriate textured background.

4 Placing the heads in the layout

The department heads were placed at the top center of the first page of each department article, with a 0.125-inch bleed. Type was set in Fenice for the article headlines, in Goudy for the body text, and in the decorative font, Remedy (from Emigre Graphics) for the initial caps.

27
Creating Department Heads: 3

John Odam

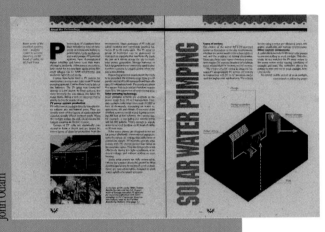

Combining a department head with a horizontal rule and decorative borders provides graphic interest and helps unify page spreads for a newsletter.

California Indian Energy News is a publication of the California Energy Extension Service, an Energy Management Action Program of the Office of Governor Pete Wilson

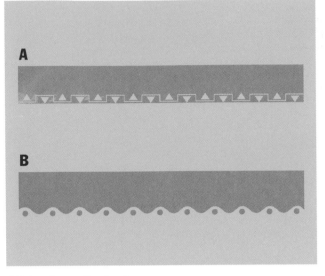

1 Using decorative borders
Designer John Odam uses a different decorative border in each issue of *California Indian Energy News*. For example, he used Aldus FreeHand to create a triangle zigzag (A) and a wave and circle design (B), both in gray. (Both could be created in PageMaker using geometric shapes and type elements).

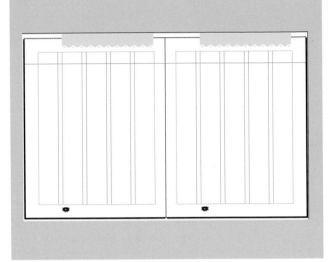

2 Positioning the borders
Odam placed a decorative border on each page of the newsletter's master page spread, positioning each so that it spanned the right 4 columns of the 5-column grid, and letting each bleed 0.125 inch off the top of the page. The borders would now appear on each page of the newsletter.

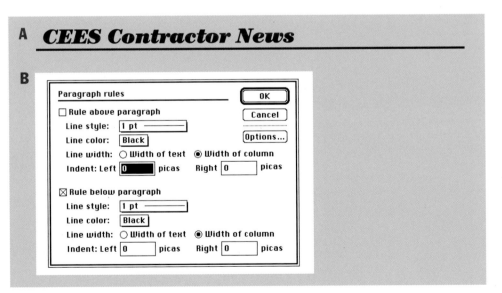

3 Specifying a paragraph rule
Each department head was set in reverse type with a 12-point black paragraph rule that provides a background. To create this, Odam first typed each title in 9-point Century Ultra italic (shown larger here) with Normal track.

He specified a 1-point rule below to run the width of the text column (A) by clicking on the appropriate buttons in the Paragraph Rules dialog box (B), available through the Paragraph Specifications dialog box.

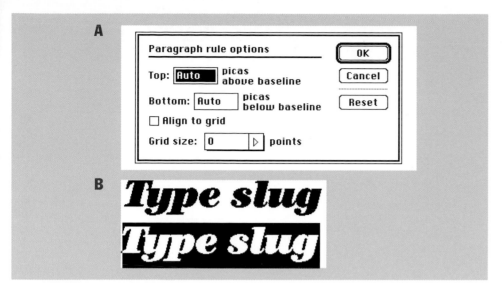

4 Setting the space below the baseline

The Paragraph Rule Options dialog box makes it possible to control how much space is inserted between the rule and the baseline of the type. Odam left these settings at their default value of Auto (A), which places the bottom of a Rule Below Paragraph at the bottom of the type "slug." The slug includes the line of type and its vertical spacing, or leading. It is the area that is highlighted when a line of text is selected, shown here in an example with Auto leading (B).

5 Changing the weight of the rule below

Changing the line weight of the paragraph rule to 6 points made it "grow" 6 points up from its baseline below the line of type (A). Changing the weight to 12 points increased the thickness of the rule until it covered the type (B). Odam changed the type specification to Reverse, to produce white type on a black background (C).

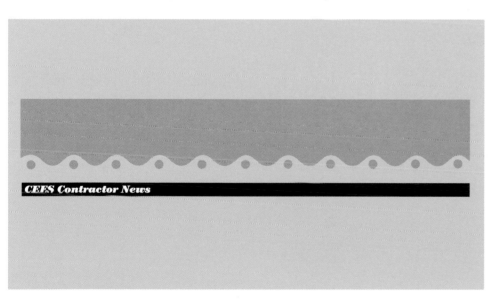

6 Combining elements

To complete the department head, Odam placed the title line below the decorative border on each page. He could then extend the text line to the same width as the border by dragging its right handle to the right.

7 Placing the heads in the layout

On the newsletter's opening spread Odam placed a department head below each decorative border, adapting the head on page 2 to fit the format of the page (which includes the masthead) by shortening it to run the width of the column of text below it. He dragged the head on page 3 to the width of the decorative border and the 2 columns of text under it. To unify 2-page article spreads, Odam pulled the department head line of type across the gutter to span both pages (see opening art).

28

Making a Type Specimen Book

You can make a type specimen book, similar to the ones typesetters once supplied, to show the entire character set of a font, to help you mix and match typefaces from those you have available, and to display the font's built-in spacing. The pages described here start with a template that comes with Page-Maker 5.0 and include pages modified from a design by Phil Gaskill.

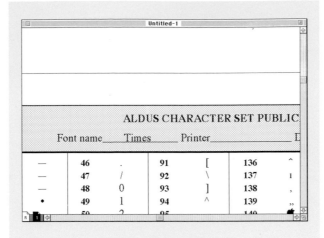

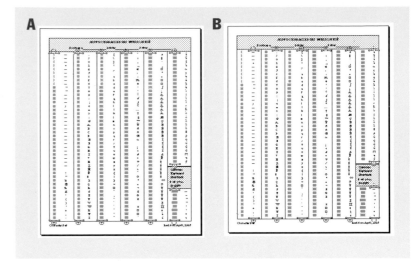

1 Starting with the Character Set template

It took 20 minutes to set up a 3-page type specs template that can generate new type sample pages almost instantly. We started with the Character Set page that comes with PageMaker 5. If you don't have it, you can make a template according to the description in the next step.

2 Looking at chart organization

Save the file under a new name, such as "Type Book," choosing Template in the Save Publication As dialog box. Note that the page shows the characters for 255 possible character assignments that exist in a standard font. The character identification numbers were typed in a single text block that was positioned to flow along the left side of each of the page's 6 vertical columns (A); the text block with the characters themselves fills the right sides of the columns (B).

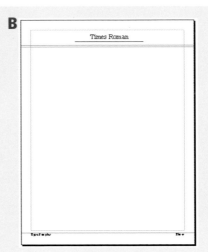

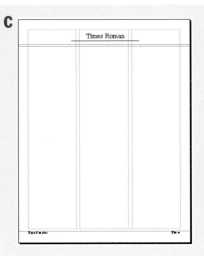

3 Formatting the specimen pages

At the top of the page, we selected and removed the header (A). On the Master page we typed the name of our first typeface (Times Roman) in 24-point Times with a Paragraph Rule After (B). We also set up 3 columns (C). ⌘ *You can set column guides on the master pages (for a whole publication), or on individual pages. To select Column Guides from the Layout menu, Guides must first be chosen from the Guides And Rulers submenu of the Layout menu.*

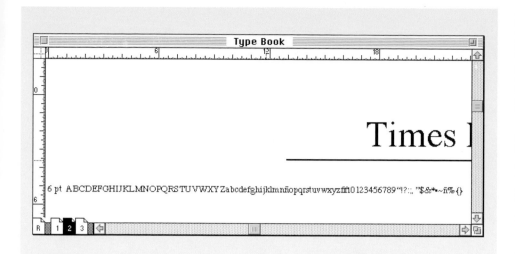

4 Adding a page for alphabet settings

We chose Insert Pages from the Layout menu to add 2 pages. Then we began setting the type. Working on the first new page with a text block that spanned all 3 columns, we chose 6 points for the type size. Near the top of the page, working with flush left alignment, we typed "6 pt" then 2 spaces, then the alphabet in caps and lowercase, and finally numbers, punctuation marks, and symbols. In the Paragraph Spacing dialog box we added a 0.25-pica Space After.

5 Adding another size

We selected this line of type with the type tool and copied it. To start a new line we placed the cursor at the end of the first line of type and pressed Return. Then we pasted the type from the clipboard. We selected the "6" and changed it to "8," and then selected the entire line and changed its size to 8 points. We would now add more single lines of type to show the relative widths and heights of the type at increasing sizes.

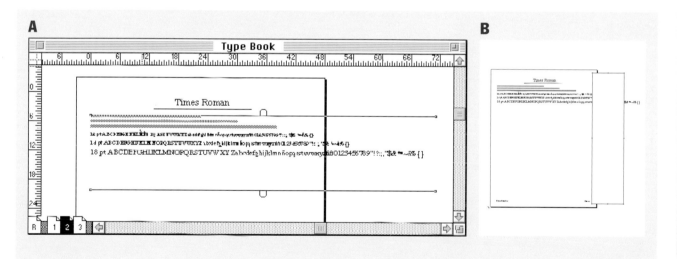

6 Adding more sizes

We continued to paste from the clipboard, following the procedures in step 5 until we had set type at 6, 8, 9, 10, 12, 14, and 18 points; we increased the Space After for the larger sizes. With the selection tool we dragged the right top handle of the text block to the right and off the page until the lines of type at the larger sizes were fully extended (A). Part of the text block hung off the page, so we covered it with a rectangle with a Fill of Paper and a 0.5-point Line to create a right margin (B).

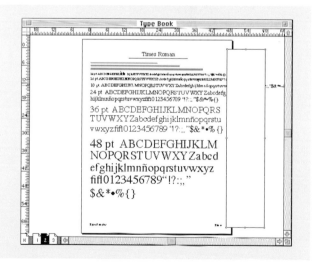

7 Adding the larger sizes

For each size sample above 18-point (24, 36 and 48 points), we typed until the text reached the visible edge of the margin block and then pressed Shift-Return to start a new line without starting a new paragraph. We continued to increase Space After; for 36-point, for example, we used 1 pica. When all the samples were set, we changed the Line of the margin block to None.

A

8/8

Tobias Hobson was the first man in England that let out hackney horses. — When a man came for a horse, he was led into the stable, where there was a great choice, but he obliged him to take the horse which stood next to the stable door; so that every customer was alike well served according to his chance, from whence it became a proverb, when what ought to be your election was forced upon you, to say "Hobson's Choice."

B

8/8.5

Tobias Hobson was the first man in England that let out hackney horses. — When a man came for a horse, he was led into the stable, where there was a great choice, but he obliged him to take the horse which stood next to the stable door; so that every customer was alike well served according to his chance, from whence it became a proverb, when what ought to be your election was forced upon you, to say "Hobson's Choice."

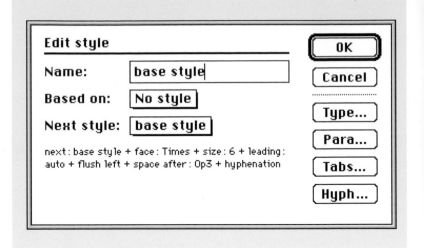

8 Adding text samples

On page 3 of the file we used the 3 columns individually to set type at 12 common size/leading combinations. We set the block (a paragraph from *Bartlett's Familiar Quotations*) at 8/8 points and labeled it with the size (A). Then we selected it with the type tool, copied it, clicked to make a new text block, and pasted it in. We changed the size (to 8/8.5) and the label (B). We continued to paste in type, sizing it at 8/9, 9/9, 9/9.5, 9/10, 10/10, 10/11, 10/12, 11/11, 11/12, and 11/13.

9 Defining a base style

We wanted to set up paragraph styles so we could quickly change all the type samples to a new face. We started by establishing a style on which all the others would be based: We clicked with the text cursor to place the insertion point in the 6-point alphabet on page 2. We held down the Command key and clicked on No Style in the Styles palette. This opened the Define Styles dialog box with a style definition based on the 6-point paragraph, which we named "base style."

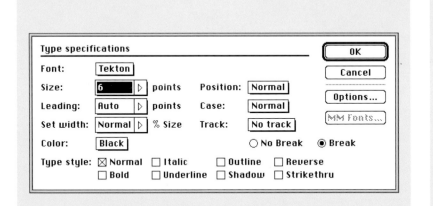

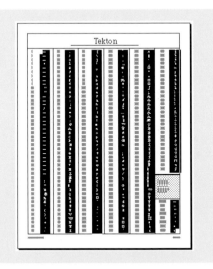

10 Defining the other styles

For each type paragraph on pages 2 and 3, we put the insertion point in a paragraph, held down the Command key and clicked No Style in the Styles palette. We chose "base style" for the Based On setting and named the style with the point size (for the samples on page 2) or the size and leading (for page 3). We added settings for the headings and footers on the master pages and for the labels. We saved the file as a template.

11 Changing the typeface on pages 2 and 3

Once we had set up the paragraph styles, it was easy to produce new type samples. We opened the template and Command-clicked on "base style" in the Style palette. When the Edit Style dialog box opened, we clicked the Type button and then chose a new font. Because all the styles on pages 2 and 3 are based on "base style," this single adjustment changes all the type samples.

12 Changing page 1 and the headings

On page 1, we clicked with the type tool to put the insertion point in 1 column of characters. Pressing Command-A selected the entire text block; then we chose the new typeface from the Font list. On the master page we changed the name of the face in the title and the footer.

#		#		#		#		#		#	
1	—	46	.	91	[	136	^	181	µ	226	â
2	—	47	/	92	\	137	ı	182	¶	227	ã
3	—	48	0	93	]	138	,	183	·	228	ä
4	•	49	1	94	^	139	„	184	‚	229	å
5	—	50	2	95	_	140		185		230	æ
6	—	51	3	96	`	141	›	186	º	231	ç
7	—	52	4	97	a	142	‹	187	»	232	è
8	—	53	5	98	b	143	‰	188		233	é
9	—	54	6	99	c	144		189		234	ê
10	"	55	7	100	d	145	'	190		235	ë
11	"	56	8	101	e	146	'	191	¿	236	ì
12	—	57	9	102	f	147	÷	192	À	237	í
13	—	58	:	103	g	148		193	Á	238	î
14	—	59	;	104	h	149	ƒ	194	Â	239	ï
15	/	60	<	105	i	150		195	Ã	240	
16	—	61	=	106	j	151	…	196	Ä	241	ñ
17	—	62	>	107	k	152	†	197	Å	242	ò
18	—	63	?	108	l	153	‡	198	Æ	243	ó
19	—	64	@	109	m	154	™	199	Ç	244	ô
20	—	65	A	110	n	155	Ÿ	200	È	245	õ
21	—	66	B	111	o	156	fi	201	É	246	ö
22	—	67	C	112	p	157	fl	202	Ê	247	
23	—	68	D	113	q	158	Œ	203	Ë	248	ø
24	—	69	E	114	r	159	œ	204	Ì	249	ù
25	—	70	F	115	s	160		205	Í	250	ú
26	—	71	G	116	t	161	¡	206	Î	251	û
27	—	72	H	117	u	162	¢	207	Ï	252	ü
28	—	73	I	118	v	163	£	208		253	
29	—	74	J	119	w	164	¤	209	Ñ	254	
30	—	75	K	120	x	165	¥	210	Ò	255	ÿ
31	—	76	L	121	y	166	/	211	Ó		
32		77	M	122	z	167	§	212	Ô		
33	!	78	N	123	{	168	¨	213	Õ	**Common Keyboard Shortcuts**	
34	"	79	O	124	|	169	©	214	Ö	O=Option	
35	#	80	P	125	}	170	ª	215		S=Shift	
36	$	81	Q	126	~	171	«	216	Ø		
37	%	82	R	127		172	¬	217	Ù		
38	&	83	S	128	ˇ	173		218	Ú	OS+=	—
39	'	84	T	129		174	®	219	Û	O+-	–
40	(	85	U	130	˒	175	˜	220	Ü	O+[	"
41	)	86	V	131		176	°	221		OS+[	"
42	*	87	W	132	˘	177	±	222		O+]	'
43	+	88	X	133	ˇ	178	˘	223	ß	OS+]	'
44	,	89	Y	134	˜	179	˝	224	à	O+8	•
45	-	90	Z	135	˙	180	´	225	á	O+6	§

8/8
Tobias Hobson was the first man in England that let out hackney horses. — When a man came for a horse, he was led into the stable, where there was a great choice, but he obliged him to take the horse which stood next to the stable door; so that every customer was alike well served according to his chance, from whence it became a proverb, when what ought to be your election was forced upon you, to say "Hobson's Choice."

8/8.5
Tobias Hobson was the first man in England that let out hackney horses. — When a man came for a horse, he was led into the stable, where there was a great choice, but he obliged him to take the horse which stood next to the stable door; so that every customer was alike well served according to his chance, from whence it became a proverb, when what ought to be your election was forced upon you, to say "Hobson's Choice."

8/9
Tobias Hobson was the first man in England that let out hackney horses. — When a man came for a horse, he was led into the stable, where there was a great choice, but he obliged him to take the horse which stood next to the stable door; so that every customer was alike well served according to his chance, from whence it became a proverb, when what ought to be your election was forced upon you, to say "Hobson's Choice."

9/9
Tobias Hobson was the first man in England that let out hackney horses. — When a man came for a horse, he was led into the stable, where there was a great choice, but he obliged him to take the horse which stood next to the stable door; so that every customer was alike well served according to his chance, from whence it became a proverb, when what ought to be your election was forced upon you, to say "Hobson's Choice."

9/9.5
Tobias Hobson was the first man in England that let out hackney horses. — When a man came for a horse, he was led into the stable, where there was a great choice, but he obliged him to take the horse which stood next to the stable door; so that every customer was alike well served according to his chance, from whence it became a proverb, when what ought to be your election was forced upon you, to say "Hobson's Choice."

9/10
Tobias Hobson was the first man in England that let out hackney horses. — When a man came for a horse, he was led into the stable, where there was a great choice, but he obliged him to take the horse which stood next to the stable door; so that every customer was alike well served according to his chance, from whence it became a proverb, when what ought to be your election was forced upon you, to say "Hobson's Choice."

10/10
Tobias Hobson was the first man in England that let out hackney horses. — When a man came for a horse, he was led into the stable, where there was a great choice, but he obliged him to take the horse which stood next to the stable door; so that every customer was alike well served according to his chance, from whence it became a proverb, when what ought to be your election was forced upon you, to say "Hobson's Choice."

10/11
Tobias Hobson was the first man in England that let out hackney horses. — When a man came for a horse, he was led into the stable, where there was a great choice, but he obliged him to take the horse which stood next to the stable door; so that every customer was alike well served according to his chance, from whence it became a proverb, when what ought to be your election was forced upon you, to say "Hobson's Choice."

10/12
Tobias Hobson was the first man in England that let out hackney horses. — When a man came for a horse, he was led into the stable, where there was a great choice, but he obliged him to take the horse which stood next to the stable door; so that every customer was alike well served according to his chance, from whence it became a proverb, when what ought to be your election was forced upon you, to say "Hobson's Choice."

11/11
Tobias Hobson was the first man in England that let out hackney horses. — When a man came for a horse, he was led into the stable, where there was a great choice, but he obliged him to take the horse which stood next to the stable door; so that every customer was alike well served according to his chance, from whence it became a proverb, when what ought to be your election was forced upon you, to say "Hobson's Choice."

11/12
Tobias Hobson was the first man in England that let out hackney horses. — When a man came for a horse, he was led into the stable, where there was a great choice, but he obliged him to take the horse which stood next to the stable door; so that every customer was alike well served according to his chance, from whence it became a proverb, when what ought to be your election was forced upon you, to say "Hobson's Choice."

11/13
Tobias Hobson was the first man in England that let out hackney horses. — When a man came for a horse, he was led into the stable, where there was a great choice, but he obliged him to take the horse which stood next to the stable door; so that every customer was alike well served according to his chance, from whence it became a proverb, when what ought to be your election was forced upon you, to say "Hobson's Choice."

13 Printing the book

We saved the file as a Document, opened our "Type Book" template again, and produced another set of pages using a different typeface, Tekton. We repeated this process until we had all the type samples we wanted. Then we used PageMaker's Book command to queue all the documents to print. We did not include page numbers on the pages because we wanted to order the typefaces alphabetically by name, and we planned to insert others into the book later, which would have dis-rupted a page numbering scheme. Shown here are examples of pages 1 and 3 from the Tekton file in our type book. Page 1 lets you see any unusual characters included in the font. Page 3 lets you compare relative character counts between text sizes. By comparing page 3 for 2 or more similar fonts, you can gauge the difference in character count between faces. (Page 2 is shown on the opening page of this chapter.)

29

Spacing Type

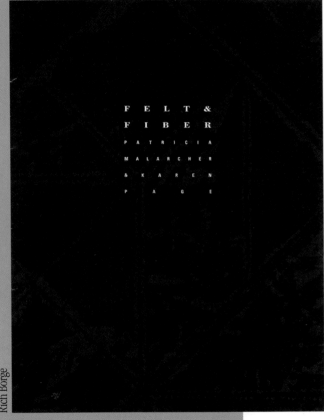

Rich Borge

Letterspacing and leading can set the "color" of a text block. Combining widely spaced type with additional white space can create pages in which text and graphics are arranged in balanced compositions of positive and negative space.

1 Typing the cover title
For the cover of an exhibit catalog, designer Rich Borge began by setting the exhibit title in 15/31-point Bodoni Bold and specified a Set Width of 120 percent in the Type Specs dialog box to widen the letters. He set the artists' names in 8.5/31-point Univers 57 Condensed.

2 Applying Force Justify
To spread the letters into a square block, Borge dragged the right corner handle of the text block to the 2.25-inch width he wanted and then selected the type with the text tool and chose Alignment, Force Justify from the Type menu. This spread the letters to fill the width of the text block.

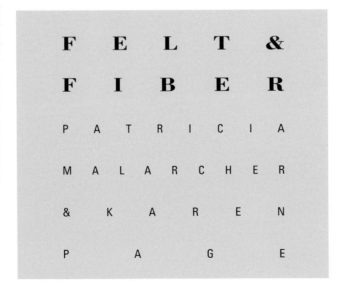

3 Adjusting the first line
The Force Justify function applied a very wide space between the 2 words in the first line. To make the letters of the first line spread more evenly, Borge inserted the cursor between each pair of letters in the first word and pressed the spacebar, so the program treated each letter as a separate word.

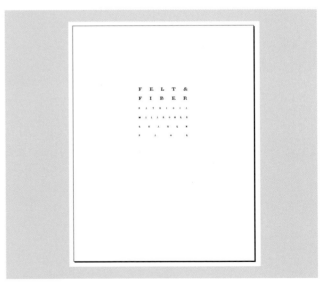

4 Creating a cover page
To create a mechanical for the printer, Borge centered the title text block, in black, near the top of an 8.5 x 11-inch page in PageMaker (above). He then directed the printer to reverse these letters out of a textured 2-color background that was supplied separately (see opening art).

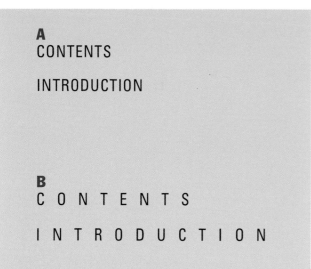

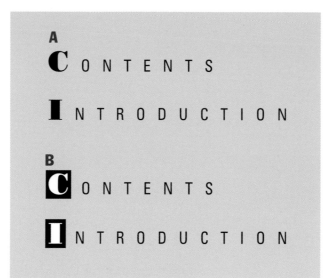

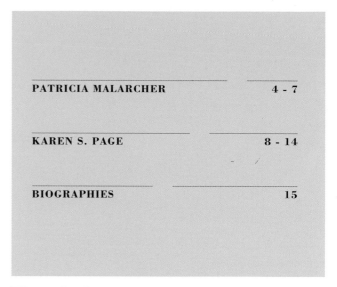

5 Creating subhead titles

To create titles for the catalog's table of contents and introductory text, Borge first typed the letters in 18/20-point Univers 57 Condensed Bold in Small Caps and applied a Set Width of 90% and a Very Loose track (A). He then spread the letters by typing 2 spaces between the letters of each pair (B).

6 Creating decorative initial capitals

To create decorative caps for each of the titles Borge selected the first letter of each and changed its Type Specifications to 22/20-point Bodoni Poster, in Small Caps, with Very Loose track (A). He then used the rectangle tool to draw a black-filled box behind each capital and reversed the initial caps (B).

7 Formatting the contents list

The contents list (shown narrower here) included only 3 items. To give it enough weight on the page, Borge set the 8-point Bodoni Bold in All Caps with a wide 20-point leading and Very Loose track. He used Indents/Tabs to align the numbers on the right and drew a hairline rule above each item.

PATRICIA MALARCHER	4 - 7
KAREN S. PAGE	8 - 14
BIOGRAPHIES	15

The issue of craft as art and art as craft is one of those chicken and egg arguments which will go on indefinitely. What is certain, however, is that the extension of media-boundary has affected all of art in this century. In fact, this may be crafts finest contribution to the dialogue surrounding craft and art. Clay, fiber, glass and metal have become shareable and interchangeable, and are no longer hierarchical or ethno-conceptual. Conversely, so called high-tech and low-tech media are now combinable. ■ Patricia Malarcher and Karen Page are two artists with craft-oriented histories and working methodologies. Both also have understood the shifting of category and media. ■ Malarcher's fiber pieces may employ the traditional techniques of brocade, applique and stitchery but they also take into account the high-tech late 20th century material of mylar (which the artist has used for 20 years). Page acknowledges her connection

8 Formatting the body text

Borge imported body text from Microsoft Word and styled it in 9/20-point Bodoni with Normal track and an alignment of Force Justify. He set the first letter of each text block in 13/20-point Univers 75 Black and applied Very Tight track to pull the second letter closer. Separating the paragraphs with a 9-point Zapf Dingbats square and running the paragraphs together created a solid block of type.

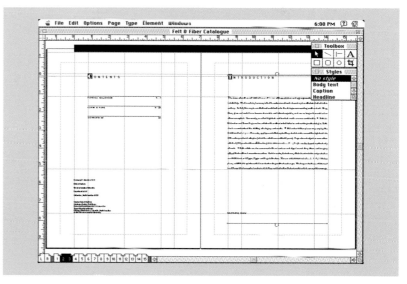

9 Laying out a spread

Borge used locked guidelines on the master pages, which he pulled from PageMaker's rulers, to create a grid that incorporates a single centered block of body text. He drew a solid black bar at the top of each page spread to span the two text blocks and visually tie the 2 pages. For the opening spread the Contents list was indented from both right and left text block margins.

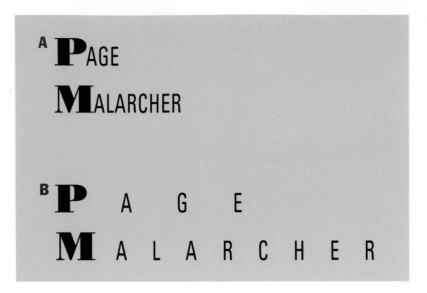

10 Condensing type with Set Width
The catalog is divided into 2 sections, each devoted to the work of a single artist. Borge set the artists' names in a style similar to that used for the Contents and Introduction titles. He began by setting the names in 20/20-point Universe 75 Condensed Bold (A) and applied a Set Width of 70% (B).

11 Spacing the titles
Borge then selected the first letter of each name and changed it to 30-point Bodoni Poster with Normal track (A). He used the space bar to insert 5 spaces between each pair of letters in the longer name and 9 spaces between each pair of letters in the shorter name (B).

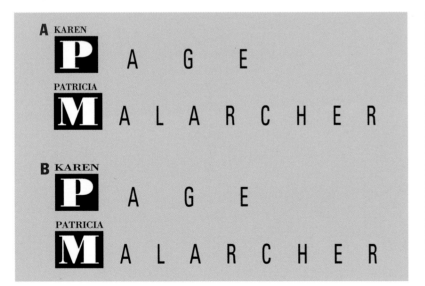

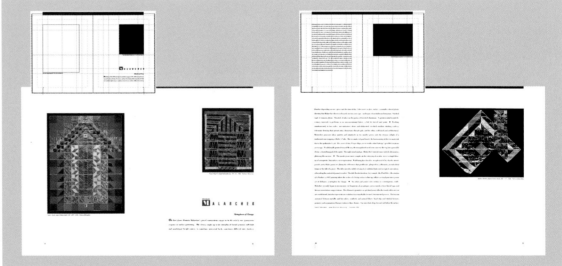

12 Creating decorative initial caps
Borge typed the first names of the artists in 7-point Bodoni in All Caps, placed each above the appropriate box (A), and then applied a Set Width value (through the Type menu or the Control palette). He experimented with widening or narrowing the letters until the width of each name matched the width of the box below it (B).

13 Laying out page spreads with a small amount of text
The commentary on the work of the first artist, Patricia Malarcher, is relatively brief. So Borge used 3 photos and a large amount of white space, spreading the text pleasingly across 2 page spreads. Folios were set off by vertical hairline rules that bled off the bottom of the page. Later the bleed was eliminated to save money on paper-trimming. Some keylines were intended to be printed; these consist of a black box with no fill. Other keylines were provided only to create a window for a photo; these consist of a box with a solid black fill.

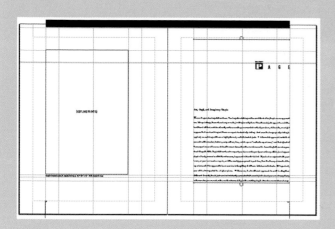
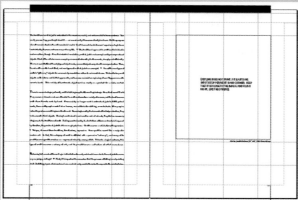
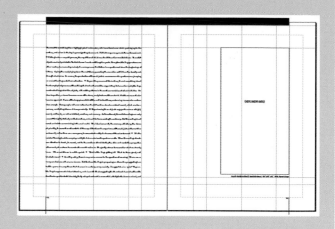

14 Laying out page spreads with a larger amount of text

The commentary on the work of the second artist, Karen Page, is longer. So Borge spread it over 3 page spreads and 1 additional page, again using 3 photographs. He continued to use the Zapf Dingbat squares to mark the beginning of each new paragraph, as in the introduction text, but for the second Karen Page spread he broke the type block into 3 sections, each of them marked off with a 1-line space and an initial cap set in 22-point Bodoni Poster. The PageMaker file included keylines for the photographs, which were stripped in later conventionally.

KAREN S. PAGE

Resides: Beaver Falls, Pennsylvania
Education: BFA Syracuse University
             MFA Kent State University
Selected awards:
             Commonwealth of Pennsylvania Council of the Arts Fellowship
             George Weaver Memorial Award, Chautaqua National Exhibition
             of American Art
Recent solo exhibitions:
             School of Art Gallery, West Virginia University
             Martha Gault Gallery, Slippery Rock University (PA)
Recent invitational exhibitions:
             Contemporary Felt Art Exhibition, Kunstnernes, Denmark
             Pennsylvania Fellowship Recipients Exhibition, Frie Art Museum and others
             Ties That Bind, Bannister Gallery, Rhode Island College
             Wool: Felted and Loomed, Textile Arts International, Minneapolis
             Points of View: A Survey of Women's Art in Western Pennsylvania,

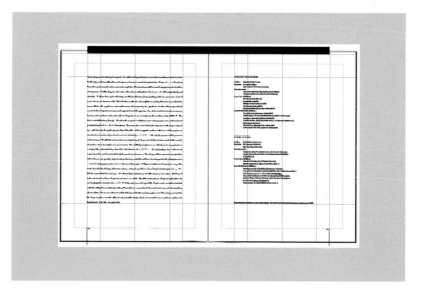

15 Formatting the artists' biographies

The last page of the catalog includes a biography of each artist, written in outline form. Borge set the artists' names in 8/10-point Bodoni Bold in All Caps with Very Loose track and drew a hairline rule above each name. He set the biographical text in 7/10-point Univers 47 Condensed Light with Very Loose track and used the Indents/Tabs dialog box to set a deep (0.5-inch) indent.

16 Finishing the catalog

The final spread includes the end of the Karen Page commentary on the left and the biographies on the right. Even without illustration, the 2 blocks of type create a pleasing composition on the spread.

30

Setting a Mood with Type

Hornall Anderson Design Works

To emphasize the theme "the art of certainty" for a service bureau's capabilities brochure, the designers at Hornall Anderson Design Works used wide leading, loose letterspacing, and white space to create pages that evoke a sense of assurance.

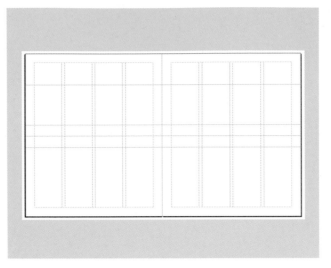

1 Setting up master pages

For the Six Sigma company's capabilities brochure, Hornall Anderson designers provided an underlying framework for the pages by setting up a 4-column grid on the master pages and included horizontal guidelines that would be used for positioning type blocks.

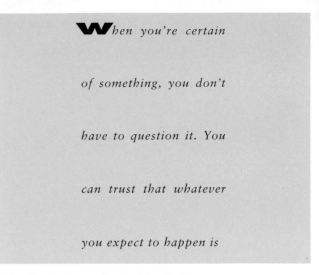

2 Setting body type for the introduction

The brochure opens with a 5-page introduction and closes with a symmetrical 5-page afterword. The body type for these sections was set in 9-point Sabon italic with a wide leading of 40 points and Very Loose track. The Alignment was set to Force Justify to spread the characters to fill the columns. An initial cap was set in 12/40-point Futura Extra Bold with a Set Width of 200%.

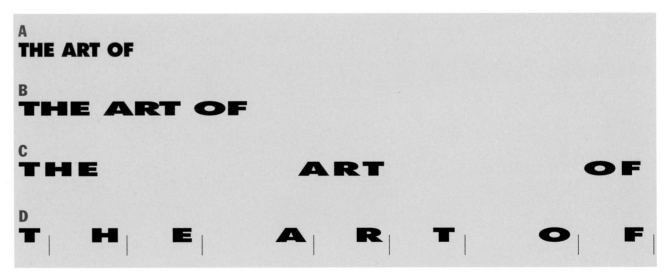

3 Setting headline type

Each 2-page spread in the brochure includes the phrase "the art of certainty" running horizontally across both pages, with the words "the art of" taking up all 4 columns on the left-hand page and the word "certainty" taking up all 4 on the right. The type was set in 14-point Futura Extra Bold (A) and then a Set Width of 200% was applied to double the width of the letters (B). The Alignment was set to Force Justify to spread the words across the 4-column-wide text block (C), and then the spacebar was used to enter a space between the letters of each pair and an extra space between words to spread the letters evenly. A short vertical 0.5-point line was drawn, copied, and positioned just to the right of each letter, using a guideline to align their bottom ends (D).

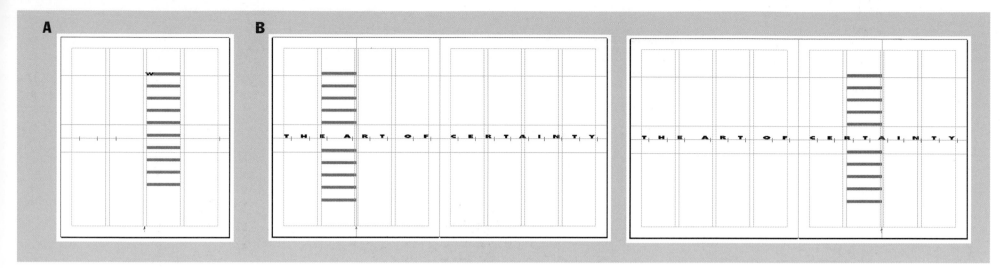

4 Setting a mood with page design

The opening page of the introduction includes only a single column of black body type along with a decorative arrow at the bottom of the page and 4 of the same short vertical lines used with "the art of certainty" title. The lines establish a sense of horizontal movement that leads the reader to the next page (A). The 2 following spreads include only 1 column of body type each, this time in red, a decorative arrow, and "the art of certainty" title, which was copied from a copy kept on the pasteboard (B). The guides were used for positioning the top of the body text block and the title, and to guide breaking the text into 2 segments as it jumps over the title. The 2 columns of type were widened slightly to prevent the last line of each from turning over to a partial line. The designer's use of a few well-placed elements composed of complementary serif and sans serif typefaces set with wide leading and letterspacing, plus a generous amount of white space, gives the pages a feeling of restraint, uncluttered elegance, and assurance. ● *When a text or graphic element will be used on many but not all pages of a document, rather than place it on the master pages, store a copy of it in an object library and retrieve copies when needed by using the Library palette.*

5 Setting body type for the center spreads

Type for the interior spreads of the brochure was set with the same specifications as for the introduction (9/40-point Sabon, Very Loose track) but was spread to a 2-column width, again with an Alignment of Force Justify. An initial cap was set in 40/40-point OPTI Bank-Script and a color of either blue, green, gold, or red was applied.

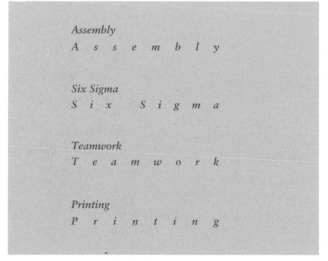

6 Formatting a page header

Each center spread includes a 0.75-inch wide header set in 8-point Sabon italic in red. Force Justify was applied to increase the letterspacing so that the word or words are spread across the type block width. Each pair above shows the type before and after the use of Force Justify. ● *Use Force Justify to spread words of varying lengths to the same column width.*

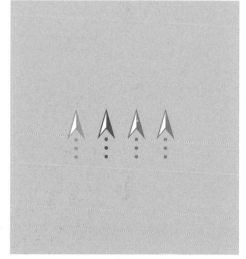

7 Replacing folios with arrows

Rather than include page numbers on each spread, the designers created a decorative arrow in Aldus FreeHand, in 4 different color versions. An arrow was imported and positioned on each spread to align with and anchor the inside edge of each column of body text.

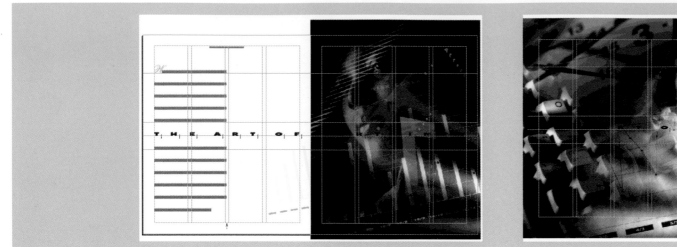
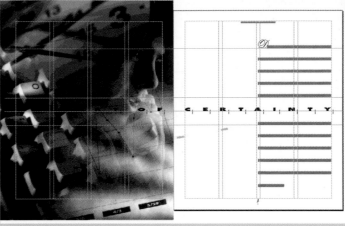

8 Laying out the center spreads

Each of the 7 interior spreads is devoted to a different topic (the 2 shown here are on Assembly and Fulfillment) and each spread was carefully composed to create a sense of refinement and reliability. The copy was carefully written to fit the page design so that each spread includes either 10 or 11 lines. When necessary, the designers sometimes asked the copywriters to add or delete text to fit the space available. The title type "the art of certainty" was positioned to print over the full-bleed photo montage on each facing page, providing a link between the pages of each spread. The photo montages were created by Seattle photographer Tom Collicott. They incorporate his photographs of FreeHand charts and graphs created by the designers and printed on a variety of textured papers. Collicott's final color transparencies were scanned as grayscale TIFFs and used as placeholders in the PageMaker layout for the purposes of screen viewing and proofing. The complete design team for the project included art director Jack Anderson, designers Heidi Hatlestad and Bruce Branson-Mayer, and copywriter Pamela Bond.

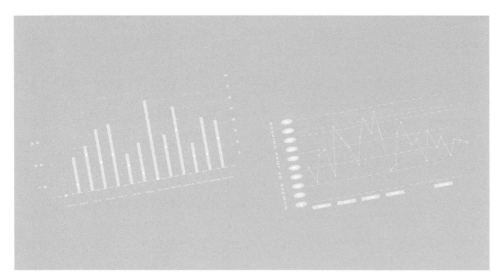
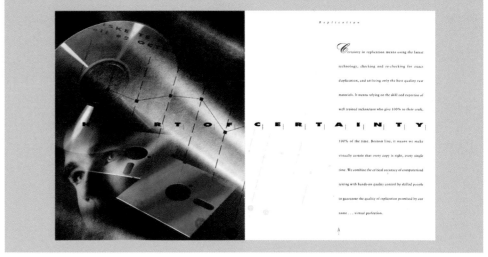

9 Linking the spreads with graphics

A series of FreeHand diagrams link the full-page montage and the type on the facing page, and were placed as EPS files in PageMaker. They were positioned on the type page of each interior spread so that they seem to be flowing out of the same diagram used in the photo montage (see step 8).

10 Printing the brochure

The final PageMaker files were sent to a service bureau that used a Scitex system for compositing the type elements with high-resolution scans of the full-color photo montages.

31

Setting Fractions

Typesetting fractions involves choosing the kind of fraction you want to set and then either selecting and reformatting each part of the fraction in turn or running a PageMaker script to do the formatting automatically.

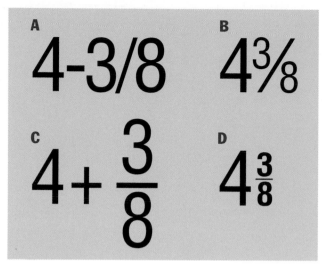

1 Recognizing common types of fractions

There are several kinds of typeset fractions: solidus (A), piece (B), built-up (C), and case (D). The kind of fraction used is often a combined design and editorial decision. ● *If you do not have the Addition or scripts required for setting fractions automatically, you can set them by following the descriptions in step 5 (for piece fractions) or step 9 (for case fractions).*

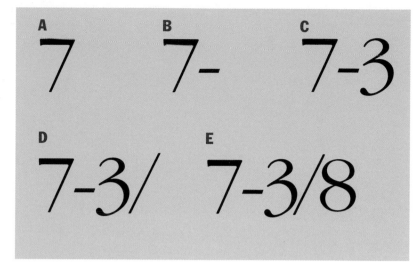

2 Setting solidus fractions

Solidus fractions are typically used in text only when there is no other easy solution. Since the other kinds of fractions are quite easy to set in PageMaker, solidus fractions need be used only for specific design purposes or as a starting point for making piece or case fractions. You can set a solidus fraction by typing the whole number (A), then a hyphen (B), then the numerator, or top part of the fraction (C), then the solidus, or slash (on the "?" key) (D), and the denominator (E).

Tired of the same old paper airplane designs? To make a **Straw Plane** you'll need:

• A strip of paper $^{15}/_{16}$ inch x $3^{15}/_{16}$ inches long

• A strip of paper 1 inch x $5^{15}/_{16}$ inches long

• A plastic drinking straw

• Clear tape

1. Make a loop out of each strip of paper, overlapping the ends and taping them both on the inside and on the outside, to make a pocket into which you can slip the straw.

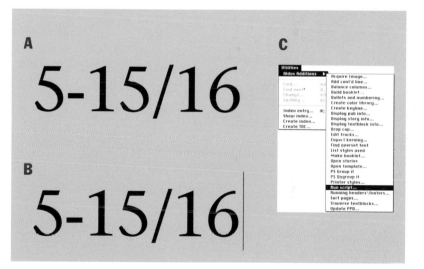

3 Using piece fractions

Piece fractions look like miniature solidus fractions. But because they are obviously fractions, they do not have to be distinguished from the whole number by a hyphen. Piece fractions are the kind most commonly used within text, recipes, and so on. The Fraction script and the Run Script Addition, both of which come with PageMaker 5.0, make it easy to set piece fractions.

4 Using the Fraction script

To set piece fractions automatically, type the fractional number as you would a solidus fraction (A). Click to insert the type cursor immediately after the last number in the denominator of the fraction (B). Then choose Run Script from the Aldus Additions submenu of the Utilities menu (C). Choose the Fraction script. ● *Once you set up a piece fraction, you can copy and paste it where you need other fractions; then select the individual numbers and type new ones.*

A

$$5\text{-}15/16$$

B

$$5\text{-}15/_{16}$$

C

$$5\text{-}15\!/_{\!16}$$

D

$$5\text{-}{}^{15}\!/_{\!16}$$

E

$$5{}^{15}\!/_{\!16}$$

F

$$5{}^{15}\!/_{\!16}$$

5 Converting to a piece fraction

The Fraction script uses the following process; if you don't have the script, you can carry out the steps by selecting parts of the fraction and applying the same changes through the Type Options dialog box: Starting with the solidus fraction (A), Fraction selects the denominator and makes it a subscript 58% of the font size and with a 0% Position setting (B). Then it selects the slash and changes it to the fraction slash (Shift-Option-1), which makes the fraction print compactly (C).

Finally, the numerator is selected and changed to a superscript at 58% of font size and 33% Position (D). If your fraction included a whole number, remove the hyphen (E). The Fractions script kerns automatically. If you need to adjust kerning to bring the parts of the fraction closer together, insert the type cursor and press Command-Delete; to move them apart, use Command-Shift-Delete. With some typefaces you may want to make the numerator and denominator (but not the slash) bold (we did not) or change their Set Width (we used 90% for this Palatino) (F).

If we wish to obtain the mean of all the samples, we must divide the sum of the values for all the samples by the number of samples:

$$m = \frac{10.24}{25} = 0.4$$

A

$$10.24$$

B

$$10.24$$
$$25$$

C

$$\frac{10.24}{25}$$

D

$$m = \frac{10.24}{25} = 0.4$$

E

$$m = \frac{10.24}{25} = 0.4$$

6 Using built-up fractions

Built-up fractions are built from numbers at the full text size. They are used almost exclusively in display settings of mathematical copy. For setting extensive display equations, it is probably worthwhile to use a specialized program such as MathType. But to set fairly simple built-up fractions, you can use PageMaker 5.0's type and line tools and the PS GroupIt Addition.

7 Setting a built-up fraction

Start a new text block and choose a typeface (we used Times). Choose Center alignment from the Type menu. Type the numerator (A) and then press Return and type the denominator (B). Use the line tool to draw the rule between the 2 parts (C). Use the pointer tool with the Shift key to select both the text block and the rule, and choose PS GroupIt from the Aldus Additions sub-

menu of the Utilities menu. This will turn the fraction into an encapsulated PostScript graphic that can be copied and pasted as an inline graphic (D), which can then be repositioned by adjusting with the Baseline Offset control in the Control palette or cropped with the crop tool (E). ❡ *Hold down the Command key to turn the crop tool into the hand tool, to adjust the position of a cropped graphic within the cropping frame.*

An *improper fraction* is a fraction whose numerator equals or is greater than its denominator. For example, $\frac{4}{4}$ and $\frac{7}{4}$ are improper fractions. An improper fraction can be *reduced* to a whole number or a whole number and a proper fraction. For instance, $\frac{4}{4}$ can be reduced to 1, and $\frac{7}{4}$ can be reduced to $1\frac{3}{4}$. Find an improper fraction that can be reduced to $128\frac{1}{4}$.

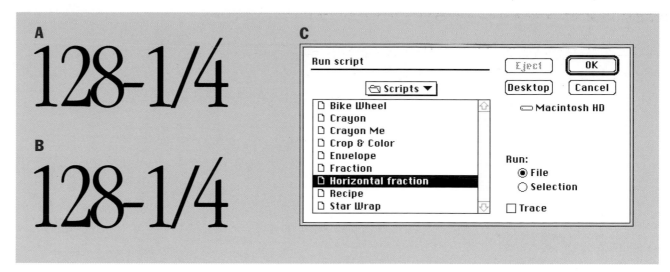

8 Using case fractions

Case fractions, often used in mathematical copy, are so called because in the days of metal type the common fractions (such as $\frac{1}{2}$, $\frac{1}{4}$, and $\frac{3}{4}$) were precast and available in the type case. The Horizontal Fraction script and the Run Script Addition, both of which come with PageMaker 5, make it easy to set case fractions with numerator and denominator between 0 and 9.

9 Using the Horizontal Fraction script

A case fraction can be set as a built-up fraction and turned into an EPS graphic (see step 7), and can be reduced after being placed as an inline graphic. But to set case fractions automatically, type the fraction as you would a solidus fraction (A). Click to insert the type cursor immediately after the last number in the fraction (B). Then choose Run Script from the Aldus Additions sub-menu of the Utilities menu (C). In the Run Script dialog box, choose Horizontal Fraction.

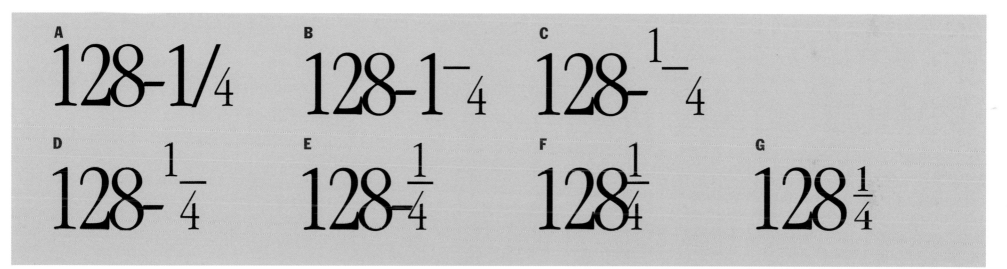

10 Converting to a case fraction

The Horizontal Fraction script uses the following process. If you don't have the script, you can carry out the steps by selecting parts of the fraction and applying the same changes through the Type Options dialog box: Horizontal Fraction selects the denominator and makes it a subscript 55% of the font size and a Position setting of 0% (A). Then it selects the solidus and changes it to the underscore character (Shift-hyphen), which is made a superscript at 55% of normal font size at a Position setting of 54%, just slightly less than the size percentage (B). The numerator is selected and changed to a super-script, also at 55% of the font size but with a Position setting of 55% (C). Then it kerns the denominator and the underscore (D). Finally it kerns the underscore and the numerator (E). If you started with a fraction that in-cluded a whole number, select the hyphen and remove it (F). The best set-tings for percentage of font size and position will vary with the font, as will kerning, weight, and set width. We made adjustments: For the 72-point Garamond Light Condensed fraction we used 40% size, superscript positions of 39% (underscore) and 40% (numerator), positive kerning between the "8" and the fraction, and Book weight and Set Width of 115% for the fraction (G).

32

Creating a Book Title Treatment

John Odam

A carefully crafted type design for a book title helps sell the book. Designer John Odam used PageMaker's type editing capabilities to create a custom title, which he varied for use on the book cover, title page, and chapter opener pages.

A Cultural Anthropology

B Cultural Anthropology

1 Setting and adjusting the type

To create a title treatment for a book on cultural anthropology, designer John Odam began by setting the type in 2 lines in 60-point Janson text, centered, with Auto leading and Normal track (A). To bring the lines closer, Odam specified a negative leading of 48 points (B). ⚹ *Negative leading is that which is smaller in point size than the point size of the type.*

A CULTURAL ANTHROPOLOGY

B CULTURAL ANTHROPOLOGY

2 Changing the case and track

To change the uppercase and lowercase letters to small capitals, Odam chose Small Caps from the Case pop-out menu in the Type Specifications dialog box (A). He then changed the track from Normal to Very Tight, to bring the characters closer together (B).

A CULTURAL ANTHRᵒPOLᵒGY

B CULTURAL ANTHRᵒPOLᵒGY

3 Converting characters to superscripts

To add interest, Odam selected the first and third "O's" in "Anthropology" and used the Type Specifications dialog box to give them a Type Style of Underline and a Position of Superscript, with default settings for superscript size and position (A). He then decreased the point size of the "O's" to 52 points so that their tops would align with the tops of the other letters in the word (B).

OLᵒGY

OLᵒGY

CULTURAL ANTHRᵒPOLᵒGY

4 Kerning the superscript

To tighten the typographic design, Odam inserted the cursor between the "L" and the third "O" and typed Option-Shift-Delete to decrease the space between the 2 letters until the superscript "O" was nested in the space above the foot of the "L."

5 Adding color and a rule below
Odam added color to the title by choosing from PageMaker's Pantone color library through the Edit Color dialog box. He used the Paragraph dialog box to add a 0.5-point black Rule Below, setting it to run the width of the column. He set the position of the rule at 3 points below the baseline. To produce a rule above the title, Odam inserted a blank line above the type by positioning the cursor to the left of the first letter and pressing Return to insert a line with no characters.

6 Finishing the title page
To complete the title page Odam added a subtitle in 24/23-point Janson italic with Normal track and then added the author's name, institution, and publisher in Janson small caps and normal (A). Though only 1 typeface is used, the different type styles and colors provide variety (B).

7 Creating a chapter opener
Odam used the same type style he had used for the title page to create titles for each of the book's chapter opener pages. Title type is set in white, with additional type in black. Imported texture scans provide borders.

8 Creating a book cover
For the book cover, Odam created a single-line variation of the 2-line title page treatment, using the same superscript specifications for the two "O's" in "Anthropology." The cover photograph was edited in Adobe Photoshop to look more like a painting; the finished cover is shown at the left.

33

Typesetting Simple Tables

Assets				
Finance receivables less fees (Consumer)	$ 3,558	$ 3,429	$ 3,332	$ 3,106
Finance receivables less fees (Commercial)	2,634	2,796	2,546	2,003
	6,182	6,225	5,878	5,109
Equipment held for lease	1,062	995	912	909
Assets held for sale	282	232	202	36
Other assets	765	768	965	241
	$ 8,286	$ 8,220	$ 7,957	$ 6,295
Liabilities and Equity				
Notes on loans payable	$ 6,590	$ 6,548	$ 6,173	$ 5,467
Other liabilities	768	876	546	975
Equity	1,567	1,453	986	788
	$ 8,915	$ 8,877	$ 7,705	$ 7,230
Revenues	$ 8,764	$ 7,652	$ 5,467	$ 4,529
Expenses				
Operating expenses	$ 614	$ 765	$ 456	$ 873
Interest	459	543	452	(78)
Income taxes	126	58	97	566
	$ 1,189	$ 1,259	$ 995	$ 1,361

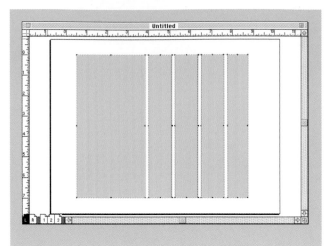

1 Planning the table format

Before you begin to enter or import data for the table, use the column guides or filled rectangles on the master pages of your PageMaker file to create an on-screen view of how the table will be formatted. Check your data to determine the number of columns and approximate column widths you will need.

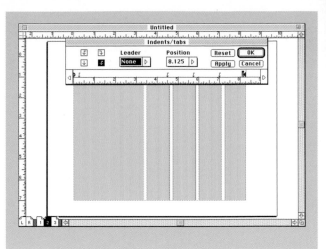

2 Setting up a text block for a table with single-line entries

Click on a page icon to move into the document; the master page elements will show up on this page. Set up a single text column the width of the entire table, and work in Fit In Window view to set the tabs for aligning the data you will enter into the table. The Index/Tabs ruler matches the rulers for the pasteboard window, so you can align the Index/Tabs dialog box and set the tabs in place by eye or by typing their positions in inches.

Rose Varieties

Far and away the most popular class of rose is the Hybrid Tea. It outsells all other classes combined. Thousands of varieties are known, and many new ones come out each year. No other flowering shrub is so widely grown. Here is a listing of some of the most popular varieties.

NAME	COLOR	FRAGRANCE	DISEASE RESISTANCE	COMMENTS
Charlotte	Red to deep pink	Lightly fragrant	Good resistance	Generally adaptable to various climates; best color in warmer areas. Reliable, heavy producer. Well-shaped buds.
Chrysler Imperial	True red	Fragrant	Resistant; some mildew	Well-foliaged. Not at its best in cool fog. Extreme weather changes hinder opening of the blooms.
Etoile de Hollande	Very dark red	Very fragrant	Moderate resistance	One of the best older roses. Good for cutting. Works well in climbing form also. Generally adaptable to various climates.
Mister Lincoln	Dark red	Strong damask	Good resistance	Buds are shapely; large flowers open flat. Generally adaptable.
Oklahoma	Black-red	Very fragrant	Good resistance	Large, urn-shaped buds. Generally adaptable, but not at its best in cool areas.
Mojave	Orange yellow, veined red	Very fragrant	Generally resistant; some mildew	Long-stemmed roses excellent for cutting; long buds also. Generally adaptable.
Tropicana	Reddish orange	Very fragrant	Highly resistant	Heavy producer of medium-sized flowers that are good for cutting. Grows upright.

The method you use to set tables in PageMaker can vary according to the kind of information the table contains.

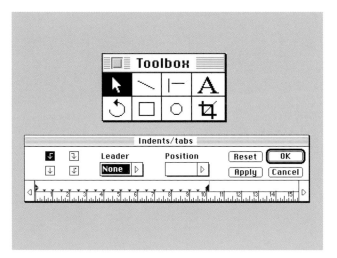

3 Setting and styling the tabs

To set the tabs, use the pointer tool, selected in the toolbox; settings made when the pointer tool is active will apply to all paragraphs you type until you reset the tabs. PageMaker provides several tab formats: left-aligning, centering, right-aligning, and decimal-aligning. Styles for tabs can be changed by selecting each individual tab and clicking on the icon for the type of tab.

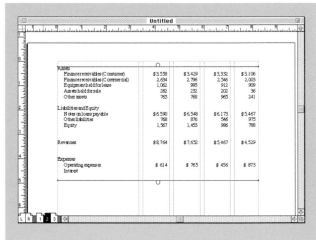

4 Entering the data

Type the data, pressing the Tab key between entries. (Alternatively you can import the data from a word-processing or database program with the tabs already in place, or type the tabs once the text is imported).

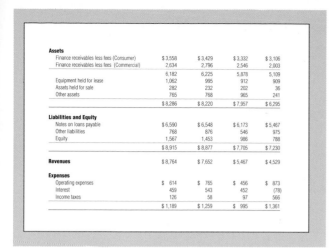

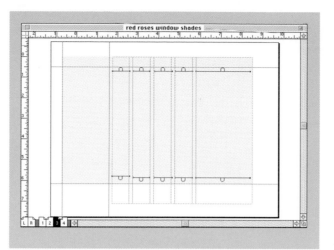

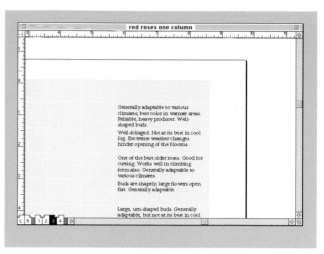

5 Styling the text

When you have completed the entries, use paragraph styles to style the type. Keep it simple: a single typeface in bold and regular will often provide enough variety. Condensed faces can help to fit more information in a narrow space. If your table needs horizontal rules, you can add them as Rule Above Paragraph or Rule Below Paragraph settings in the Paragraph Rules dialog box. These rules will travel along with the text if you edit the table.

6 Setting up text blocks for a table with multi-line entries

If some columns of your table contain long entries that will require more than one line of the table, you can set each column as a separate text block.

7 Entering the largest block of text

First type the entries for the column that will contain the most lines of text, using paragraph returns only between entries. Then style this text, adjusting the leading and space between paragraphs so the text fits the height of the table.

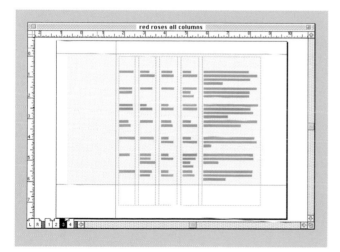

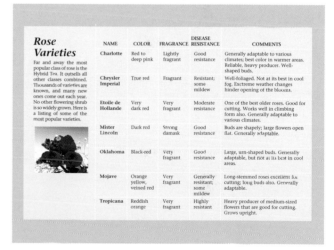

8 Completing the other columns

Use guidelines and the snap-to-guides feature as well as the leading setting in paragraph styles to align the text in the other columns with the text in the column you finished.

9 Styling column heads

To get a clear, good-looking table, build column widths according to the table entries themselves, not the column headings. Then adjust the column heads to fit. Heads can be stacked (as shown here) or even set at an angle or abbreviated, if necessary, to make them fit over their columns.

10 Making things clear

When the table is complete, use space, rules, or tints to help visually organize it. You can draw a horizontal rule and use the program's Multiple Paste function to repeat it, adjusting positions as necessary. Or size a color block to fit 1 row of the table, and then select alternate rows and change the color, using light tints that will not interfere with readability. Whenever possible, accompany the table with a clear explanation of its contents.

34

Combining Colors

PageMaker's Define Colors function makes it easy to create and use an infinite number of hues, tints, and shades. Defining a color adds it to the Colors palette, where it can be easily selected and applied. Color wheels and triangles can be used to generate color combinations that work well to create different moods and styles.

1 Creating a black-and-white design
We began by creating a type design in black and white. With a good composition and balance between positive and negative values, a simple design can be effective. The typefaces used were, from the top, Adobe's Zapf

Dingbats (for the star) and Cheltenham, and Emigre's Remedy and Elektrix. Next we inverted the colors in the design to produce a negative version.

2 Creating a grayscale variation
A grayscale version of the design mixes tints of varying percentages of black. Tints can be created by clicking on Tint in the Define Colors dialog box, available from the Element menu.

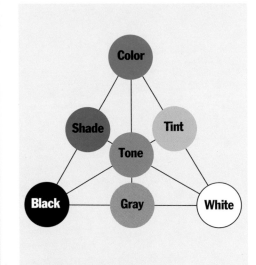

3 Using a color triangle
A color triangle describes the relationships between shades (colors mixed with black), tints (colors mixed with white), and tones (colors mixed with gray).

4 Creating and using tints
To create tints of blue for this version of the design, we clicked on Tint in the Edit Color dialog box (from Define Colors from the Element menu) and specified percentage values of a single base color.

5 Creating shades and tones
We added black to the original blue to create shades (A). To make tones, we added gray by first adding black and then decreasing the color components of the blue, which effectively added "white" (B).

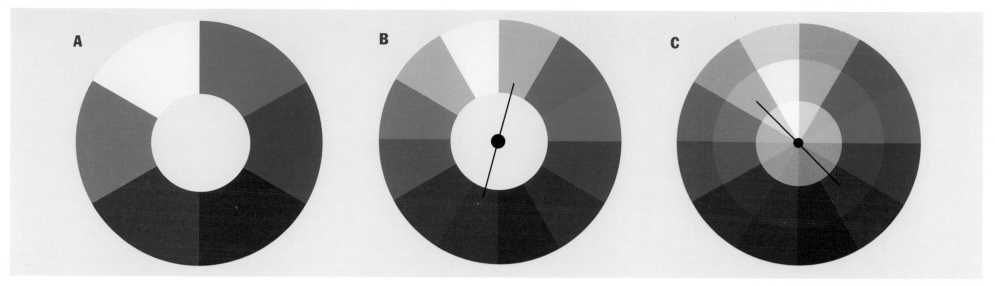

6 Working with a color wheel

In a color wheel hues are arranged around a circle in the order they appear in a rainbow. In a basic wheel of 6 colors (A), based not on screen displays or process printing inks but on traditional paint pigments, the primary colors (red, yellow, and blue) alternate with secondary colors (orange, green, and violet). A color wheel with smaller subdivisions of color, like this 12-color version (B), can be used to determine pairs, triads, or larger groups of colors that will produce pleasing combinations . For example, colors that are directly opposite each other on the wheel are called *complements* and can be used effectively together.

Adding white or black to hues produces tints and shades respectively. A 3-part color wheel (C) can be used to help locate groups of colors, tints (the inner circle includes 50% tints of the colors), and shades (colors in the outer circle have been darkened with 15% black), and that will work well together. We used Aldus FreeHand to create the color wheels on this page.

7 Combining complementary colors

We have varied the color in a single type illustration to demonstrate the different color combinations and show how different colors affect the mood of a piece. These 2 examples show the use of complementary colors. The colors in this and the following examples were chosen from the 12-color wheel shown in step 6.

8 Combining near complementary colors

A pleasing group of 3 colors can be created by combining a color with the two colors on either side of its complement. These are called *near complements*.

9 Combining double complements
Pairs of complementary colors can be combined to produce groups of four colors that look harmonious together.

10 Combining triadic complements
Pleasing combinations can also be created by choosing 3 colors that are equidistant from each other around the color wheel.

11 Combining multiple complements
Multiple complements are groups of 5 colors that are adjacent on a 12-color wheel.

12 Using pastels
Another way to produce pleasing color combinations is by combining colors that have similar tint values. Here we have created 2 combinations in pale, pastel tints.

13 Using muted tones

Muted, or grayed, tones can be combined effectively. Here we have used warm gold and red tones and cooler tones of blue. Instead of adding black and then subtracting color to "add white," you can increase the percentage of the smallest component (cyan, magenta, or yellow).

14 Combining brights with neutral tones

Highly muted, or neutral, tones, including grays and muted tones of color, create an effective balance when combined with bright, highly saturated colors.

15 Setting off brights with black

Bright colors look even brighter when set off by black. Black can be used either for foreground subjects or as a background.

16 Combining brights, neutrals, and blacks

Another combination that produces a rich color feeling is that of muted, neutral tones with black and accents of bright color.

35

Illustrating with PageMaker's Drawing Tools

Roots & Wings

You can create sophisticated and attractive illustrations for your publication using the simple line, rectangle, and ellipse tools available in PageMaker.

Janet Ashford

Drawing with straight lines

We used the line tool to draw a tree beginning with a heavy 12-point line weight for the trunk and changing to lighter and lighter line weights as we moved outward to the thinner branches. An enlarged detail is shown here.

Selecting and grouping the lines

To group the lines we dragged the pointer tool around the construction to select all the lines, and then chose PS GroupIt from the Aldus Additions submenu of the Utilities menu.

Copying and flipping the tree

We copied the grouped tree, selected a point at its bottom, opened the Control palette, and clicked on the Vertical-reflecting button to flip the copy.

Adding the birds

We used the line tool to draw the shape of a bird. We grouped the bird, made several copies, and positioned them to complete the illustration.

Drawing with ellipses and rectangles
We started this illustration by drawing a basic structure of overlapping ellipses and rectangles. Each shape was specified with a solid color fill and no outline.

Adding detail
We added realism to the illustration by adding details to the windows, shutters, house wall, tree and other elements, using the ellipse, rectangle, and line tools.

Viewing the structure
A keyline view of the illustration (all shapes have been specified with a black line and no fill) shows the construction of the clouds, tree, bushes, and other elements.

Overlapping shapes
Dramatic illustrations can be created by overlapping simple shapes. The winding road was created by layering a green ellipse over a light gray ellipse.

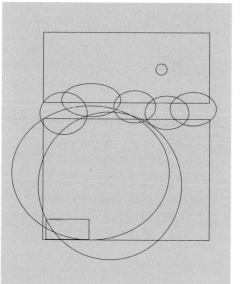

Viewing the structure
A keyline view shows the simple structure of the winding road illustration.

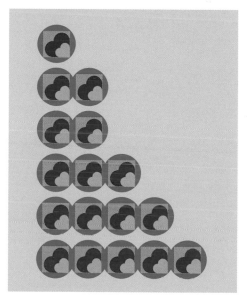

Creating the basis for a tiled pattern
We used the drawing tools to create a tile made of circles and squares.

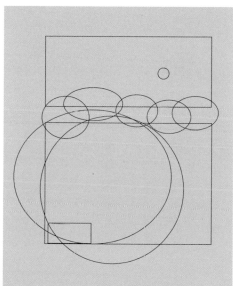

Using Multiple Paste
We grouped the tile elements, selected the tile group and used Multiple Paste to copy and offset it into a row of 5.

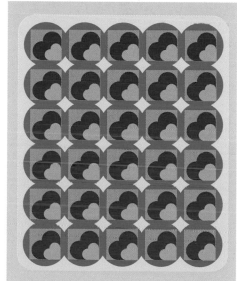

Creating a grid
We selected and grouped the row of 5 tiles, used Multiple Paste to produce a grid of 6 rows, and then added a solid background.

Creating a collection of shapes

We created various shapes and patterns with the ellipse, rectangle, and line tools. We used the Fill And Line dialog box from the Element menu to color the shapes.

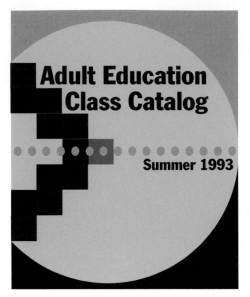

Combining shapes to create designs

We combined shapes and patterns to produce abstract designs.

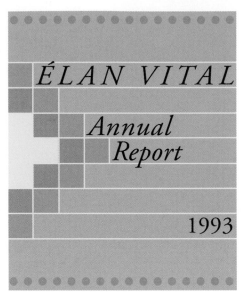

Varying the palette

We experimented with both strong and pastel palettes.

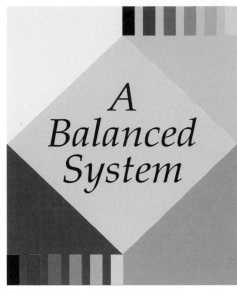

Working with only 2 colors

Tints of only 2 colors can produce the effect of a larger palette.

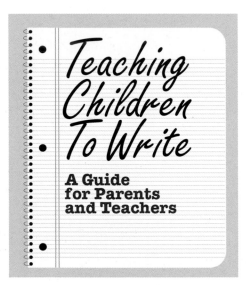

Creating a notebook with shapes

We drew the yellow paper shape with the rectangle tool, with corner shapes set through Element, Rounded Corners. Horizontal and vertical lines were made with the line tool.

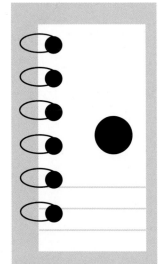

Drawing black ellipses

To make the spiral binding, we held down the Shift key to draw perfect black circles, and then drew and positioned black-line ellipses.

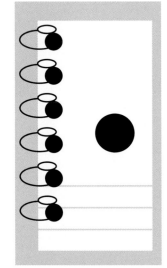

Drawing mask shapes

We drew small ellipses filled with the background color and positioned them as shown.

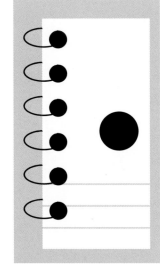

Creating an illusion

We removed the outline from the small shapes to create the illusion of spiral binding passing through the holes in the paper.

Creating a variation

We experimented to create design variations and new illustrations.

36
Using Type as Ornament

Symbol fonts contain many handsome and decorative characters that can be used as ornaments or combined and changed to create illustrations and textures.

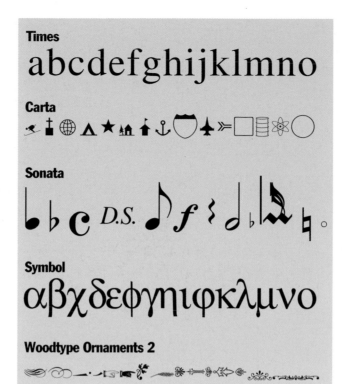

Exploring different symbol fonts
The characters of symbol fonts are created simply by typing on the computer keyboard. Several specialized Adobe fonts are available, including Carta for map-making, Sonata for music notation, and Symbol for mathematics. In addition, some fonts, like Woodtype Ornaments 2, are based on old-style printer's ornaments. We have shown the first 15 characters of each font, corresponding to the first 15 letters of the English alphabet.

Making a font chart
Zapf Dingbats is one of the most commonly used symbol fonts. To indicate which key will produce which symbol character, use PageMaker to type each line of alphabetic characters on the keyboard, then place a corresponding line of symbols underneath. Divide your chart into 4 sections — Unshifted, Shift, Option, and Option-Shift — to indicate which characters are available when these additional keys are held down. When your chart is complete, Save As and create additional charts for other symbol fonts simply by selecting each line of symbol characters and changing it to the new font. You may have to adjust the letter spacing or kerning to make each symbol character line up under the corresponding alphabet character.

Normal

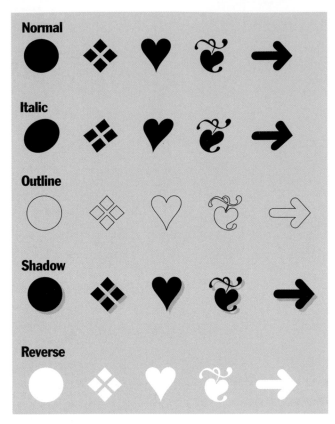

Italic

Outline

Shadow

Reverse

Applying type effects

Most of the type styles that can be applied to alphabet fonts can also be applied to symbols fonts. Shown here are Normal, Italic, Outline, Shadow, and Reverse styles.

Using other effects

You can produce interesting results by offsetting characters to produce a 3-dimensional effect or by placing characters of different sizes over each other.

Creating ornamental borders

The simplest ornamental border is made by typing a row of a single character. You can vary the size and letter spacing. We used 3 characters from the Zapf Dingbats font for these examples. A vertical border can be made by making a text block with a character on each line or by rotating a horizontal border by 90 degrees.

Alternating 2 characters

To create a more sophisticated border, experiment with combining characters from 1 font or several fonts. We alternated a leaf symbol with the bullet symbol (Option-8), and then used the line tool to add border lines. We also alternated a snowflake symbol with the vertical line character.

Adding color

You can add color to any font character simply by selecting it and clicking on a color in the Colors palette. We colored the entire row of leaves and bullets green, then went back to change each bullet to red. Use the line and rectangle tools to create backgrounds and borders.

Overlapping rows of characters

Rows of type characters can be colored and overlapped to produce interesting patterns. We placed a row of red arrows over a row of yellow half circles, both from Zapf Dingbats. We also placed a row of jagged explosion symbols from the Carta font over a row of black squares and green vertical lines.

Using a border character

Some decorative fonts, like Woodtype Ornaments 2, include symbols that are designed to be typed in a row to create an ornamental border.

Tightening letter spacing

Another way to create a pattern is by typing a row of symbols and tightening the space between them with kerning or tracking until the characters touch.

Rotating character rows

With symbols that are symmetrical across the horizontal axis, you can create two facing rows by copying 1 row and rotating it 180 degrees.

Reflecting character rows

With symbols that are not symmetrical, you can create two facing rows by using the Horizontal-reflecting button in the Control palette to flip a row.

Experimenting with variations

Both old-style and modern borders can be created by combining ornamental font characters or simple symbols and shapes.

Starting with single characters
Some symbol characters are interesting enough to use alone as ornaments.

Overlapping and combining characters
More complex ornaments and illustrations can be created by adding color to ornaments and combining them. The cityscape uses a symbol from Carta.

Rotating, reflecting, and skewing
Symbols can be combined and varied even further by using the rotate, skew, and reflect functions.

Varying color palettes
The same design can have a very different look and feel when the color palette is changed from bright, hot colors to more muted pastels.

Creating a grid of characters
Type can be used to create a decorative, textured background by typing rows of characters to make up a grid.

Adding colors
Complete the texture by adding color to the type and a solid-colored background rectangle.

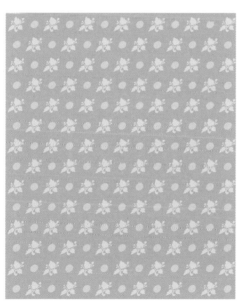

Adding a focal point
A single character can be used as a spot illustration or focal point when set in a large point size. We used the circle tool to add pink berries to the leaf symbol.

Completing the design with type
Finish the design by adding alphabetic type.

37

Framing a Photo: 1

To crop a photo to a rectangular shape on a PageMaker page is easy — just use the crop tool. To crop to an oval shape is a bit more complicated, but you can do it by making a mask with PageMaker 5's oval tool.

1 Drawing an oval
Place the photo or artwork and draw an ellipse on top of it with the oval tool. The ellipse does not have to be the size and shape you want your frame to be because you will stretch or shrink it later.

2 Thickening the border
Assign the oval a fill of None through the Fill menu and a thick line through the Custom choice in the Line menu. ✦ *Unlike previous versions, PageMaker 5 does not limit line width to 12 points.*

3 Coloring the mask
Choose Reverse Line from the Line menu if you want to frame the image against a blank part of the page. Or give the line the color of a tint block behind the image as we did for the opening art.

4 Expanding the frame
With the selection pointer, stretch or move the oval until it frames the image the way you like. The opening in the frame will enlarge as you stretch, while the framing line will stay the same thickness.

5 Tidying up the edges
If necessary, crop the photo to tuck the edges under the oval mask. Once the framing is complete, you can add 1 or more slightly larger oval lines (see opening art).

38

Framing a Photo: 2

To crop a photo to a diamond shape, you start with a square frame, thicken and stretch it, and then crop the photo if necessary, or make rectangular corners to cover any areas that extend beyond the frame but cannot be cropped.

1 Drawing a square

To crop to a diamond shape, start by drawing on top of the photo with the rectangle tool. Hold down the Shift key as you draw to constrain the rectangle to a square.

2 Rotating the square

With the square selected, click on the rotation tool in the Control palette, select the center point in the proxy box, type "45" for the degrees of rotation, and click the button.

3 Thickening the frame

Copy the frame and put the copy on the pasteboard so you can use it later to make a rule around the photo. Assign a Custom (thick) line width and a fill of None to the original frame on the photo.

4 Coloring the frame

Assign the rotated square the appropriate color, either Reverse Line (for the color of the paper) or the color of the background tint block as we used here.

5 Opening up the frame

Hold down the Shift key and stretch or move the frame with the selection pointer to frame the image. If the corners of the photo project outside the framing diamond, use the crop tool to trim the photo.

6 Adding a rule

To add a rule around the photo, retrieve the original thin diamond frame from the pasteboard, Shift-drag to stretch or shrink it if necessary, and assign it a new weight, line style, and color.

39

Layering Photos: 1

CACTUS

A single scanned image can be used to illustrate an entire page simply by scaling it, cropping it, and adding color and contrasting backgrounds.

Janet Ashford

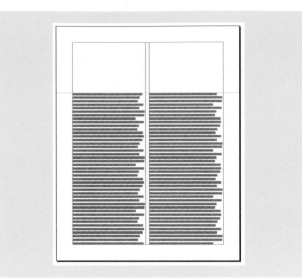

1 Starting the page
We began our page by opening PageMaker and specifying a 2-column format using the Column Guides command under the Layout menu. We entered body text and positioned it in 2 columns, beginning about a quarter of the way down the page.

2 Importing a grayscale TIFF
To create illustrations for the page we started with a scanned grayscale image of cactus. The Image Control dialog box which appeared when we selected the image and chose Image Control from the Element menu shows the smooth ramp of grayscale values in the original image.

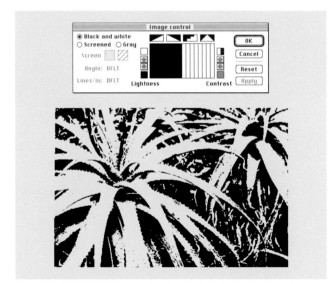

3 Converting to high contrast
First, we placed the image in the layout and made it high-contrast by using the Image Control dialog box to convert it to Black And White mode.

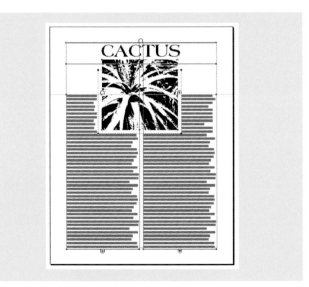

4 Cropping and positioning
We used the cropping tool to crop the high-contrast image, centered it near the top of the page and applied a Text Wrap so that the 2 columns of body type wrapped around it. We then added a headline in the Americana font.

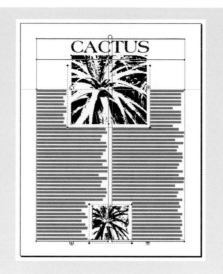

5 Inverting a high-contrast image

To create a second version of the cactus image we made a copy of the high-contrast image and clicked on the Reverse gray levels icon in the Image Control dialog box (the second icon from the left) to reverse its black-and-white values.

6 Cropping, scaling, and positioning

We reduced the size of the second image by dragging one of its corner handles, with the Shift key held down to retain its proportions, positioned it at the bottom of the page and applied a Text Wrap.

7 Lightening the image

To use same image as a background, we imported the original grayscale TIFF again and lightened it by clicking on the upward pointing arrow of the Lighten controls in the Image Control.

8 Adding a background layer

We enlarged the lightened TIFF, cropped it to the size of the page and sent it behind the other elements. ★ *Though the high-contrast TIFFs look transparent on screen, their clear areas will print as opaque white when the page is color-separated because they are not true 1-bit TIFFs but 8-bit grayscale TIFFs that have been converted to black-and-white in PageMaker.*

9 Adding color and an overprinting black

For a 2-color version we applied a blue to the background image and to a box behind the reversed image, and applied a 40 percent blue screen to a box behind the high-contrast image (see the opening art). ★ *The TIFFs look transparent on screen but to make sure they print that way, assign them a tint of 100% black set to Overprint in the Define Colors dialog box.*

40

Layering Photos: 2

Janet Ashford

Scanned black-and-white images can be imported and manipulated to create striking illustration elements for a publication. Color or tints of black can be added, and images can be made transparent to allow the use of contrasting background colors.

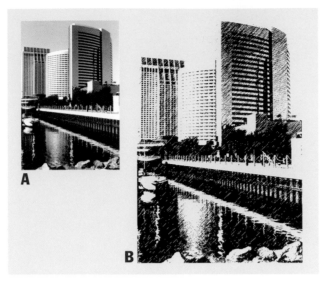

A

B

1 Importing a 1-bit TIFF

We started with a color image (A) and used Adobe Photoshop to apply an artistic effect and to convert the image to a black-and-white (1-bit) TIFF. Because the white areas of a 1-bit TIFF are transparent, the beige background of our figure box shows through (B).

2 Adding a color or tint

We placed the TIFF in PageMaker, cropped it to a central detail, and changed the black areas to medium gray by clicking on this color in the Colors palette. The color had been added to the palette by using the Define Colors command from the Element menu. We drew a rectangle, gave it a solid fill, changed its color to light gray, and placed it behind the transparent TIFF.

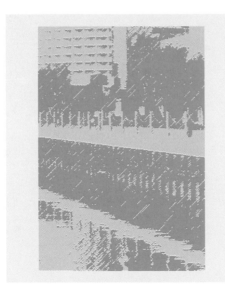

3 Creating a second 2-color image

To create a special effect we copied the TIFF detail, positioned the copy exactly over the original, then cropped it toward its center, changed its color to dark gray, and placed a pale blue rectangle behind it.

San Diego Waterfront

4 Layering a third image and type

We finished our postcard design by creating a scaled version of the uncropped TIFF in black over a medium blue background and placing it over the 2 background TIFFs. Blue type in Helvetica Ultra Compressed over a pale red band completed the design. ☻ *If your scanner supports the TWAIN interface, you can scan directly from PageMaker 5 without using an image editor such as Photoshop.*

41

Layering Front and Back Elements

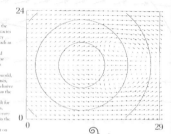

Diane Fenster

Layering foreground and background elements on a page can create a sense of depth. Designer Diane Fenster used the technique also to provide texture and graphic interest for a magazine page using a single, simple illustration.

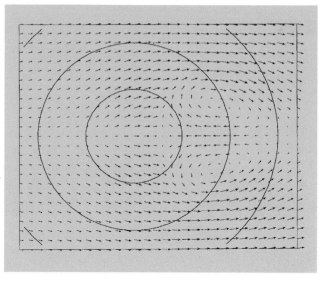

1 Starting the page

For an article for *Intersci*, a publication of the San Francisco State University School of Science, designer Diane Fenster began by setting and positioning the title, byline, department head and 2 columns of body type.

2 Scanning a graphic

To illustrate the article, Fenster scanned a diagram from a science book as black-and-white line art at 300 dpi, opened the scan in Photoshop, and sized it to fit the smaller size she expected to use in the layout, about 3.5 x 3 inches.

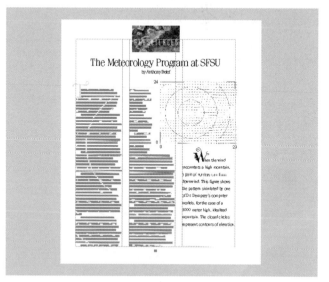

3 Wrapping text around the graphic

Fenster imported and positioned the graphic on the page and then integrated it into the design by using the Text Wrap command to make the body text wrap around it. To fill the space in the column below the graphic, she added a pull quote with a decorative initial cap.

4 Adding a second copy of the graphic

To provide a textural background for the page, Fenster copied the diagram scan, applied a 15% black tint through the Colors palette, enlarged the scan until it bled off the page, and sent it behind the other elements. Enlarging the scan reduced its resolution, but this roughness added to its textural quality.

42

Making a Duotone

A duotone is a grayscale image printed with 2 colors of ink. You can produce duotones in PageMaker by overprinting 2 copies of an imported image, varying the way color is applied to each of the two copies.

1 Importing the image

Use the Place command to import a grayscale image saved in TIFF format. The Image Control dialog box will look like this before you make any changes.

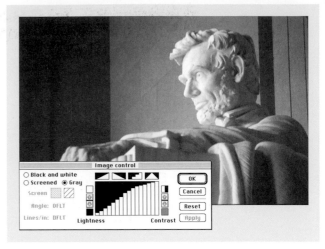

2 Assigning the first ink

With the image selected, assign the color of the first ink by choosing from the Colors palette. Then choose Element, Image Control. Adjust the settings to determine how that ink will print in the highlight, midtone, and shadow ranges by dragging the top of each white column up or down in the Image Control dialog box; or click at the level you want the bar to be. Highlights are represented at the right end of the graph, shadows at the left.

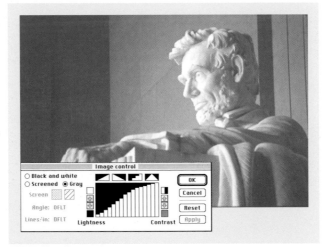

3 Cloning the image

To make a second copy of the image exactly on top of the first, use power paste: Select the image and copy it to the clipboard; then hold down the Option key while you paste it. With this new copy in place and still selected, assign it the second ink color from the Colors palette. In this case magenta is the second ink color.

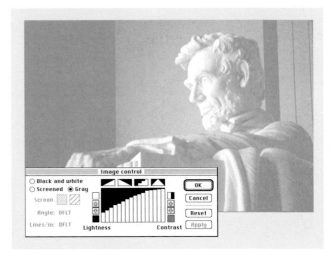

4 Adjusting the second ink color

Again select Element, Image Control and adjust the levels of the white bars. Since grayscale TIFFs are not transparent on screen, the underlying black image will not show through.

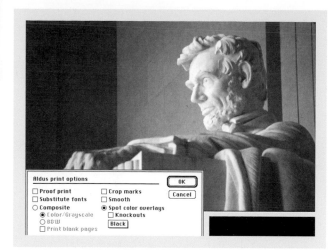

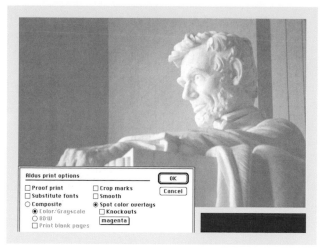

5 Setting the images to overprint

Select each of the copies of the image in turn and choose Element, Fill And Line; then choose Overprint. Before sending the file for color separation, you can test to see that it will separate properly by printing on a laser printer in black-and-white. In the Print dialog box, choose Color. Then, in the Color dialog box, select each ink color you want to print and select Print This Ink. With Overprint designated for both copies of the image in the Fill And Line

dialog box, the 2 copies should print in their entirety, 1 ink over the other, so that the 2 colors mix in the printed image. 🍎 *Instead of setting the overprinting at the object level (through the Element, Fill And Line dialog box), you can set the colors to overprint by choosing Element, Define Colors, Edit Color and checking the Overprint box. However, this causes the color to overprint everywhere it occurs in the document.*

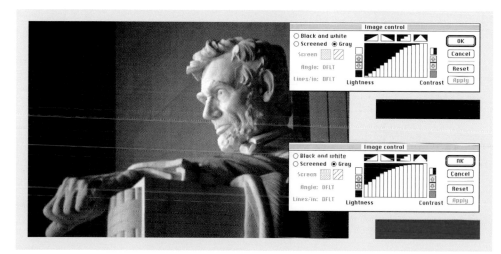

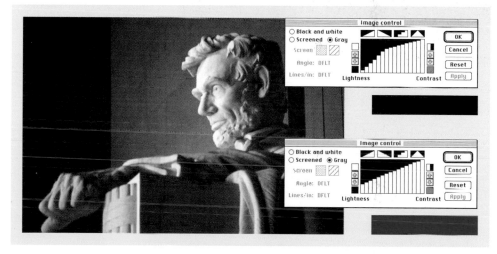

6 Experimenting with other duotone curves

Changing the settings in the Image Control dialog box can produce different results with the same inks. The second ink color may add a dramatic color effect to the image (as shown above), or its main purpose may be to add a subtle tint (above right) or to broaden the range of darks and lights that can be printed.

43

Creating Custom Screens

Janet Ashford

PageMaker's Image Control command makes it possible to override the default settings used for printing screened artwork and apply a custom line or dot screen with any screen angle and number of lines per inch. A low-resolution line screen can transform ordinary grayscale images into interesting graphics.

1 Scanning a color image

We started by scanning a color photo of cactus at 150 dpi. Image Control does not work on color images, so we would need a grayscale file. Although we could have set our scanner to make a grayscale scan, we chose to make the conversion to grayscale in Adobe Photoshop instead.

2 Converting to grayscale

After converting the image to grayscale mode, we saved it as a TIFF, and then imported the TIFF into PageMaker. Checking the Image Control dialog box (under the Element menu) when the image is selected shows its current parameters.

3 Applying a color

We used the Define Colors command to create a blue-green color, then clicked on this color in the Colors palette to apply it to the selected grayscale image. Now all the black areas of the image are rendered in blue-green, but the Image Control histogram remains the same.

4 Applying a horizontal line screen

PageMaker's Image Control defaults are set to apply a dot screen, typically at an angle of 45 degrees at 53 or 90 lines per inch. To create a custom horizontal line screen for the cactus image we clicked on Screened, clicked on the line screen icon, and entered values of 90 degrees and 30 lpi.

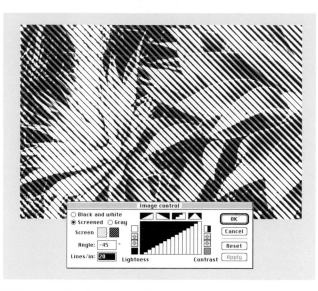

5 Applying a vertical screen

To create a vertical line screen, we entered a value of 0 for screen angle, along with 30 lines per inch. ● *Applying a line screen at a low value (from 20 to 40 lpi) can make a grayscale image look more like an engraving.*

6 Applying an angled screen

To create a diagonal screen running from upper left to lower right, we specified an angle of –45 degrees at 30 lpi. Entering a value of +45 degrees would produce a diagonal screen from lower left to upper right. An angle of any degree can be specified to produce diagonals that are more or less steep.

7 Changing the lines per inch

To make the image more dramatic, we specified a very coarse line screen at 20 lines per inch and kept the angle at –45 degrees. Creating a line screen, especially a screen that is diagonal and fairly coarse, can give a grayscale image the look of an etching.

8 Applying a coarse dot screen

Line screens are used most often for special effects, but a coarse dot screen can also be effective. We applied a dot screen at 20 lpi. ● *Applying a dot screen at a very low value such as 20 lpi can produce a "pop art" look like that used by poster artists of the 1960s and '70s.*

9 Converting to high-contrast

To create a high-contrast image, we adjusted the black and white sliders in the Image Control histogram until they were all white on the right and black on the left. We then applied a line screen at 45 degrees and 40 lpi. Unlike a 1-bit image, the white areas of this screened grayscale image are opaque.

10 Simulating a line screen

To create a 2-color image with the look of a line screen, we converted the image to black and white and then used Multiple Paste to draw a grid of equally spaced 1-point lines across the image.

44

Customizing Photos with Image Control

Janet Ashford

PageMaker's Image Control dialog box can be used to edit imported grayscale images, with gray levels that can be adjusted lighter or darker. Images can be inverted, solarized, or posterized by preset patterns or manipulated in other ways to produce custom effects. The image shown above is a 3-level posterization.

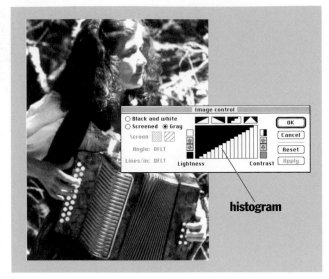

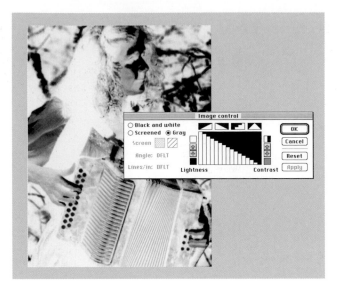

1 Importing a grayscale image
When a grayscale TIFF is imported into PageMaker and selected, the Image Control command under the Element window becomes active. The Image Control dialog box includes a histogram of 16 gray levels. Controls allow adjustment of lightness and contrast.

2 Inverting the image
Clicking on any of the four icons at the top of the dialog box changes the histogram to that pattern. The first is the normal setting for a grayscale image with a smooth ramp of values from black on the left to white on the right. The second icon inverts these values to produce a negative, as shown here.

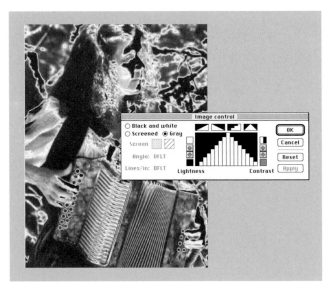

3 Creating a 4-level posterization
Clicking on the third icon creates a stair-stepped histogram in which the 16 different gray levels are converted to only 4 levels, including black, white, and 2 shades of gray. This has the effect of producing a 4-level posterization of the image.

4 Solarizing the image
A solarized image is one in which half the gray levels are normal and the other half are inverted. Clicking on the fourth icon in the dialog box produces a solarization by converting the gray levels in the histogram to a triangular pattern.

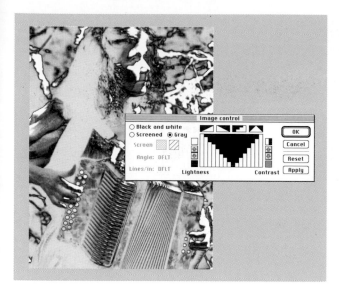

5 Creating a reverse solarization

The gray levels in the histogram can be manipulated directly to create custom patterns. Levels can be changed by dragging the white bars up and down, or by clicking at the desired location to snap the white bar to that level. We edited the histogram to produce an inverted solarization.

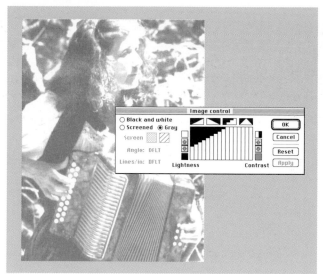

6 Adjusting brightness

Brightness can be adjusted by clicking the up or down arrow above Lightness to lighten or darken the image respectively. This raises or lowers the histogram sliders as a group, retaining whatever pattern is current. Starting with the normal pattern (step 1), we clicked the up arrow to increase brightness.

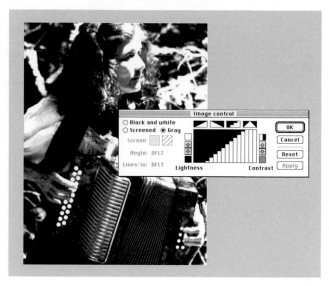

7 Adjusting contrast

We clicked on the up arrow above Contrast to make the grayscale ramp of the image steeper, thus increasing the contrast between its light and dark areas. Clicking on the down arrow makes the ramp flatter, thus decreasing the contrast by bringing the gray levels closer to the same value.

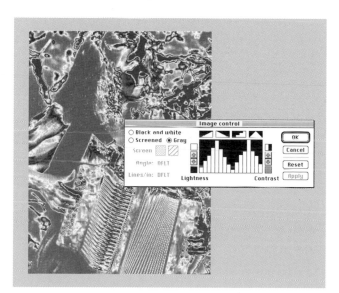

8 Creating a custom histogram

Dragging the cursor through the histogram with the mouse button depressed causes the slider bars to snap to the cursor's path. This method, or clicking once on each bar, can be used to create custom patterns like this one with 2 peaks or like the 3-level posterization shown on the opposite page.

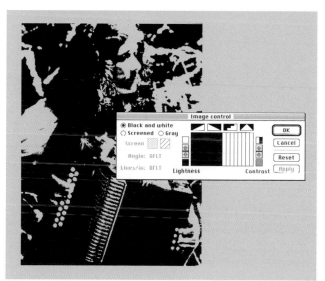

9 Converting to black-and-white

A grayscale image can be converted to a high-contrast black-and-white image by clicking on the Black And White button in the Image Control dialog box.

10 Applying a custom line screen

Clicking on Screened to convert a grayscale image to a screened image makes it possible to choose either a line or a dot screen and enter custom values for screen angle and lines per inch. We created a special effect by specifying a line screen at 25 lpi with a screen angle of 0 degrees (vertical).

Livening Up an Annual Report

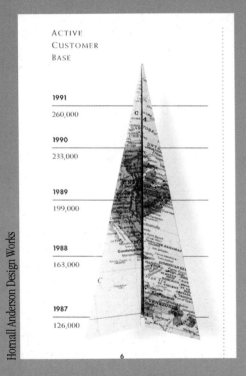

An annual report has to include pages of financial tables presented in a standard businesslike form. But for a recent Airborne Express Annual Report, paper airplanes added an elegant touch of whimsy to illustrate the narrative section.

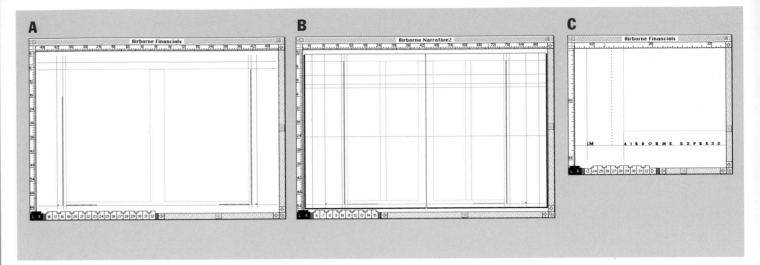

1 Setting up Master pages

John Anicker, who carried out the electronic design and production of the Airborne Express annual report for Hornall Anderson Design Works, Inc., created separate files for the different kinds of information that would be presented in the report, so he could have appropriate Master pages for each type of material. Master pages for the financial section had narrow margins; each page would be filled with a single column of tables and explanatory text (A). The narrative part of the report had 2 text columns and wider margin columns that could accommodate graphs and the expanded text blocks that would be used for sidebars (B). Master pages for all the files included a page number, a footer with the name of the company and the date of the report, and a vertical dotted line to separate a margin column from the rest of the page (C).

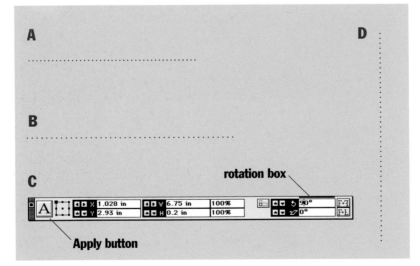

2 Customizing a dotted line

To better control the size and spacing of the dots in the margin lines, Anicker set a line of periods in Adobe's Weiss Bold font (A), and set the Track to Very Loose (B). A new angle (90 degrees) was typed into the rotation box in the Control palette, and the Apply button was clicked (C). This rotated the line into position (D). ⌘ *Another way to set a vertical dotted line is to type a period and a Return repeatedly. Then adjust the spacing by changing the Leading setting.*

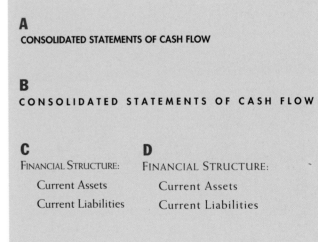

3 Spacing the type

In setting up paragraph styles for headings, the designers specified Futura (in both normal and bold) (A) and increased the Desired letterspacing from 0% to 110% to open up space between the characters (B). For the Weiss font used for text, the Small Caps height was changed from the default 70% of the caps height (C) to 80%, and the track was set at Very Loose (D).

A

B

FINANCIAL STRUCTURE:

Current Assets	$ 194,640	$ 175,939	$149,514	$ 125,899	$101,552
Current Liabilities	176,641	148,289	124,644	92,766	66,080
Working Capital	17,999	27,650	24,870	33,133	35,472
Property and Equipment	613,149	419,873	306,429	288,928	247,974
Equipment Deposits and Other Assets	15,858	17,722	14,662	7,225	6,189
Total	$ 647,006	$ 465,245	$345,961	$329,286	$289,635
Long-Term Liabilities	$ 319,662	$ 161,828	$177,835	$201,868	$165,190
Redeemable Preferred Stock	40,000	40,000	—	—	—
Shareholders' Equity	287,344	263,417	168,126	127,418	124,445
Total	$ 647,006	$ 465,245	$345,961		

4 Setting up the financial tables

On the financial pages, tables were set up using the full width of the report's 8.5 x 11-inch page. The Indents/Tabs ruler was used to set left-hand tabs for headings and subheadings and right-hand tabs for the columns of numbers; since the figures were expressed in whole-dollar amounts (to represent thousands), decimal tabs were not necessary (A). Adobe's Weiss font was set at 9/14 points for most text entries in the tables, and at 9.5/14 for the main headings and for all the numbers. The current year's figures were set in color. Hairline rules were incorporated into the tables by setting a Rule Below in the Paragraph Rules dialog box. For "Totals," the designers used a hairline Rule Above in black and a hairline Rule Below in color (B).

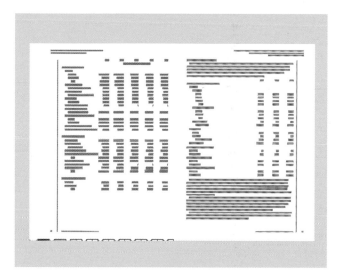

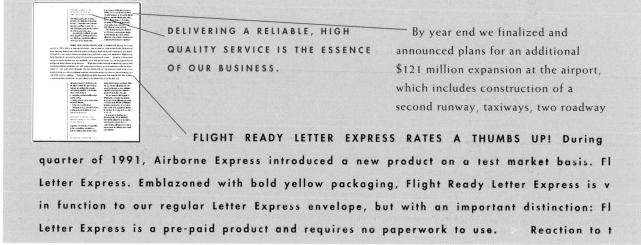

DELIVERING A RELIABLE, HIGH QUALITY SERVICE IS THE ESSENCE OF OUR BUSINESS.

By year end we finalized and announced plans for an additional $121 million expansion at the airport, which includes construction of a second runway, taxiways, two roadway

FLIGHT READY LETTER EXPRESS RATES A THUMBS UP! During quarter of 1991, Airborne Express introduced a new product on a test market basis. Fl Letter Express. Emblazoned with bold yellow packaging, Flight Ready Letter Express is v in function to our regular Letter Express envelope, but with an important distinction: Fl Letter Express is a pre-paid product and requires no paperwork to use. Reaction to t

5 Completing the financial pages

Text for the financial pages was set in Weiss in a single column. The 14-point leading added enough space between lines to maintain readability of the wide columns of 9-point type.

6 Designing the narrative pages

Within the text area of the narrative pages, Anicker set up 2 columns in which he set Weiss type on wide leading, maintaining the open feeling created by the margins and dotted lines. Headlines in Futura All Caps were set in color in 2 or 3 lines. Sidebars were set in Futura bold with added letter-spacing at the full width of the text area plus the margin column. ● *For flush left or right type, only the Desired, not Maximum or Minimum, settings in the Spacing dialog affect spacing.*

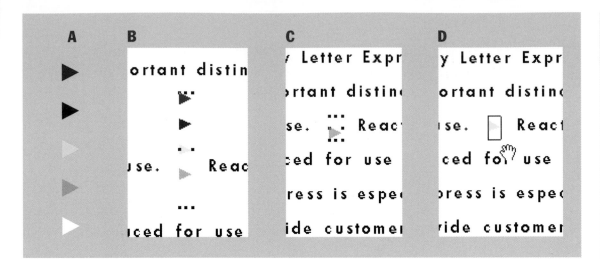

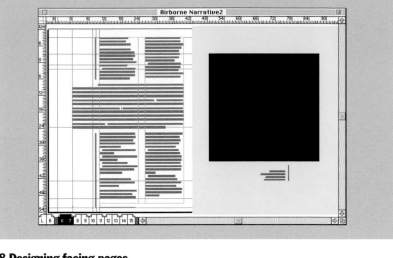

7 Importing dingbats
In the sidebar text, triangular dingbats divided the single text block into paragraphs. Anicker drew a dingbat in Aldus FreeHand, sized to fit with the sidebar type. He made 3 more copies of the dingbat, aligned vertically, in Pantone colors (A). He saved this file as an EPS. Whenever he needed a triangle, he placed the file as an inline graphic (B), cropped it to the height of a single dingbat (C), and used the Option key with the crop tool to scroll the right dingbat into view (D).

8 Designing facing pages
Most text pages in the narrative section faced a large window set to hold a place for a photo, framed in a solid block of a Pantone ink color. In his PageMaker files Anicker used spot colors to generate the film for the Pantone colors. Other elements on the photo page were a caption and an echo of the vertical dotted line, both in black.

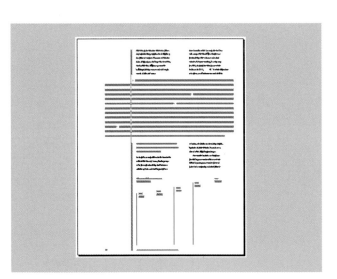

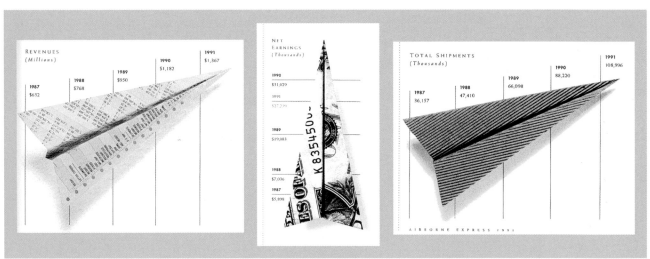

9 Laying out the graphs
To get the accuracy he needed for the number components of the graphs that would show the company's growth, Anicker used FreeHand's precise drawing capabilities. He saved the FreeHand graphs in EPS format, placed them on the PageMaker pages, traced the lines with the line tool, and then deleted the EPS's, leaving only the PageMaker elements as shown here.

10 Adding airplanes
The paper airplane provided the perfect form for representing upward movement, with a strong line in the center fold and an overall arrowhead shape. Anicker made planes in several materials, including a world map for the "Active Customer Base" graph (see opening art), a computer print-out for revenues, a dollar bill for the net earnings graph, and corrugated paper to represent total shipments. The planes and their shadows were photographed to be stripped in by the printer.

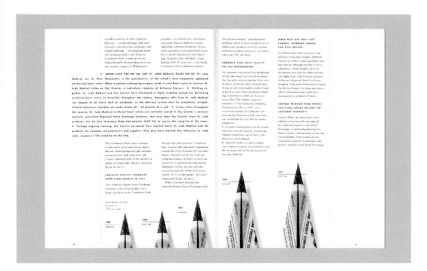

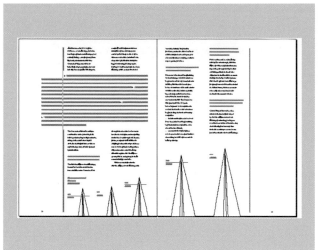

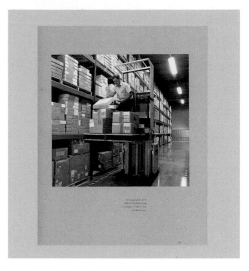

11 Illustrating a histogram

In most cases the planes were used simply to show the direction of a trend. But in the "Shareholders' Equity" graph, they were used in a histogram. The designers were aware that using larger planes to represent growing equity would be misleading, since the reader would focus on the difference in *area* rather than the difference in *height*. So they used the dark tip and dark vertical center line of a folded stock certificate as a pointer, showing more of the line as equity grew.

12 Making a proof for the printer

To indicate where the paper plane photos should be stripped in, Anicker provided the printer with laser prints that included planes he had "sketched" in FreeHand and imported.

13 Completing the narrative pages

The black-and-white photos used to illustrate the narrative section were scanned in color and printed in process color inks (cyan, magenta, yellow, and black), to emphasize warm or cool tones so that they matched the background color, which bled off the page.

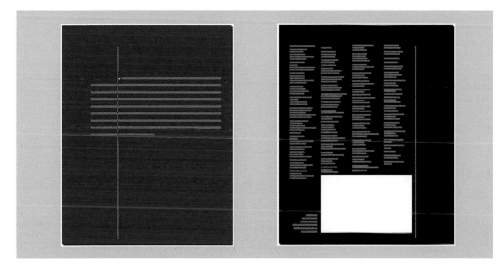

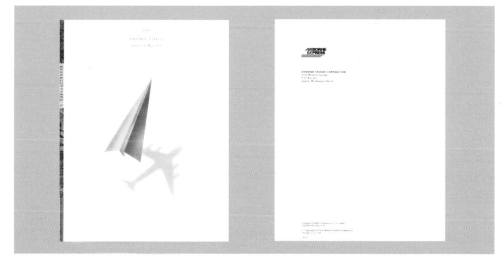

14 Designing the inside covers

The inside front and back covers included type and the vertical dotted line reversed out of red in the case of the front cover and black in the back. The introductory text on the red front cover page was set in the same typeface and at the same width as the sidebars inside. The back cover listed the directors, officers, and subsidiaries and included a place-holder for a photo.

15 Designing the covers

The cover was white with an eye-catching black-and-white airplane graphic. Wrapping the spine were swatches of the materials used to make the paper planes shown inside. On the back were the Airborne Express logo, the company's address, and employment and copyright notices. In addition to Anicker, others involved in design of the report were John Hornall and Julia LaPine (art directors), Heidi Hatlestad (designer), and Jeff Zaruba and Tom Collicott (photographers).

46

Rotating, Reflecting, and Skewing Graphics and Type

Janet Ashford

The rotation tool and the controls on the Control palette can be used to transform native graphics, imported graphics, and type by rotating, reflecting, and skewing them.

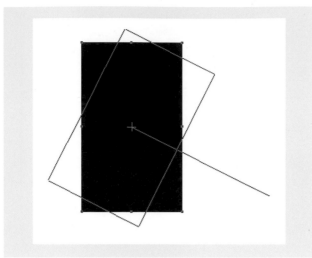

1 Rotating using the rotation tool

To rotate a rectangle we selected it and then clicked on the rotation tool in the tool palette. We clicked at the center of the rectangle to define a reference point for the rotation, then dragged the rotation lever to rotate the rectangle.

 To automatically rotate from an object's center, hold down the Command key as you click anywhere to define the reference point.

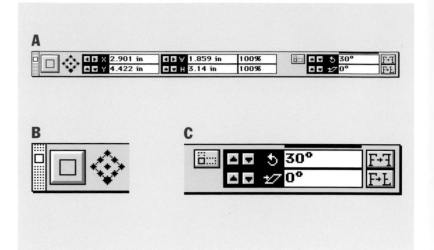

2 Rotating using the Control palette

Objects, including text blocks, can also be rotated using the Control palette (A). To rotate an object, select it and click on a point in the proxy to define a reference point for the rotation (B). Then enter positive or negative values in increments of 0.01 degrees in the rotation field in the Control palette (C). Zero degrees is at the 3 o'clock position. Positive numbers rotate objects counterclockwise while negative numbers rotate objects clockwise.

3 Rotating imported PostScript clip art

We imported a palm tree graphic from 3G Graphics' Places and Faces 1 collection of PostScript clip art (A). We copied the graphic, used the Control palette to rotate the copies in increments of 45 degrees (we used +90, –90, +45, and –45 degrees), positioned the trees around the top half of a circle, and added type and a background to create a hotel logo (B).

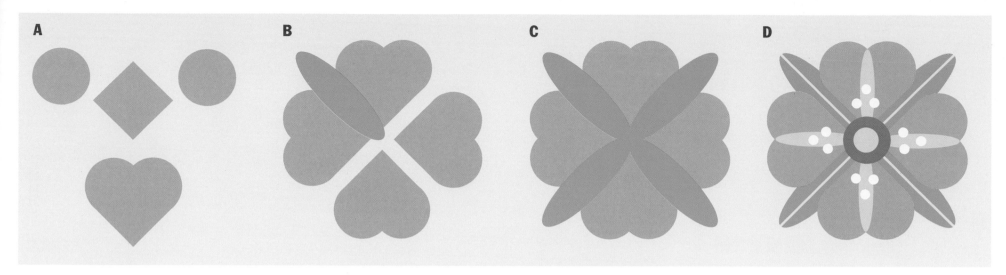

4 Rotating native graphics

The Rotation tool makes it possible to create attractive original graphics using the simple geometric drawing tools available in PageMaker. We created a stylized flower by first constructing a heart shape out of 2 circles and a square that was rotated 90 degrees (A). We selected the three objects that made up the heart, copied them three times, and rotated the copies in increments of 90 degrees to create the petals of the flower. We used the ellipse tool to draw a thin vertical oval and rotated it 135 degrees to create a leaf (B). We continued copying and rotating the leaf in 90-degree increments to create 4 leaves (C). We added more details, including rotated pink ovals on the petals, to complete the flower (D).

5 Rotating type

To create a design using type we set a block of type in Helvetica Bold, colored it tan, and rotated it about −55 degrees to slant it from upper left to lower right. We placed the block over a rectangle and masked off the overlapping type with rectangles filled with the background color. We then colored a new text block red and rotated it 35 degrees.

6 Reflecting using the Control palette

To reflect a graphic object or text block, select it and click on either the Horizontal or Vertical reflecting button in the Control palette (A). We clicked on the Horizontal reflecting button (at the top) to flip a blue rectangle and type horizontally (B). We clicked on the Vertical reflecting button to flip the same graphic vertically (C).

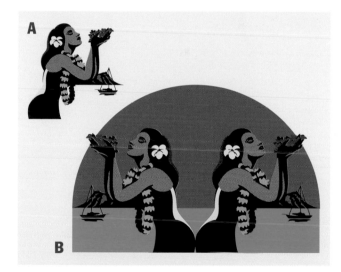

7 Reflecting imported PostScript clip art

We used the Place command to import a PostScript graphic from 3G Graphics' Places & Faces 1 collection (A). We used the Horizontal reflecting button to reflect a copy of the graphic along the horizontal axis and then added background shapes to create a new, unified graphic (B).

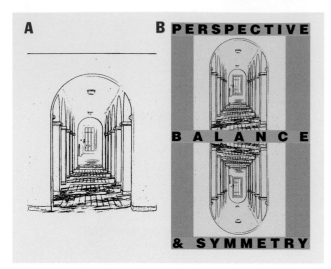

8 Reflecting an imported bitmap graphic

We imported a black-and-white bitmapped TIFF created from a photo scan in Photoshop (A). We copied and reflected the image vertically and then added type and background shapes filled with color. Because the white areas of the imported 1-bit TIFF are transparent, the background colors show through (B).

9 Reflecting type

Script type can be used to create decorative patterns. We used Shelley Allegro Script to set the word "Flowers" and reflected a copy vertically to create a mirrored pair. We copied the 2 elements and flipped the copies horizontally, then copied all 4 elements and rotated the copies 90 degrees until we had a pattern of 4 pairs. All the copies were colored beige except the one that reads correctly.

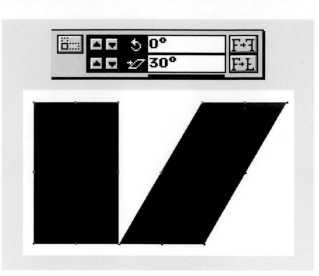

10 Skewing with the Control palette

To skew a graphic object or text block select it and enter a number value in the Skew Angle field in the Control palette. ☀ *You can also adjust number values up or down by clicking on the up and down arrows to the left of the Rotate and Skew controls. The amount of skew (or rotation) applied to the object is updated with each click.*

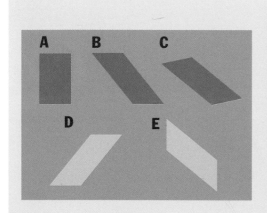

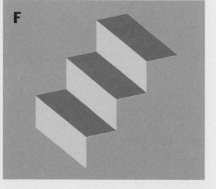

11 Skewing native graphics

To create a staircase, we first drew a rectangle (A) and used the Control palette to skew it by entering a value of 38 degrees in the Skew field (B). We copied the skewed rectangle and rotated the copy slightly to create a stair tread (C). We then copied the skewed rectangle again, flipped it horizontally, and changed its color (D). We rotated the new shape to create a stair riser (E). We then assembled copies of the tread and riser shapes to create a 3-step stair (F).

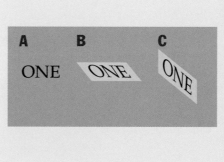

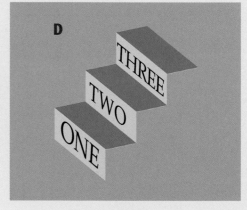

12 Skewing type

To create skewed type for the stairs we began by setting type in Palatino (A). Using a copy of 1 of the stair risers as a guide, we rotated it until its long sides were horizontal, positioned the type over it, and used the Control palette to skew the type so that its angle matched that of the sides of the stair riser shape (B). We then rotated the riser and type until the riser's short sides were vertical and positioned the riser and type in the stair (C). We repeated the process to create type for the remaining 2 stair risers (D).

47

Evolving an Electronic Approach

Fritz Klaetke

Many designers combine traditional and desktop methods to produce pages before making the transition to fully electronic production.

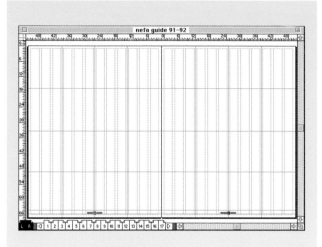

1 Setting up a multicolumn grid

To design the annual "Guide to Programs" for the New England Foundation for the Arts, Fritz Klaetke begins by setting up a 10-column grid on each of the master pages. This allows the flexibility he needs to maintain the structure of pages that vary greatly in the kinds of text and photos they will need to accommodate.

2 Designing the cover

Like many of the interior spreads, the front cover of the "Guide" includes photos that bleed off the page. For the 2 issues described here, the printer stripped in the photos and color screens by traditional methods. So the PageMaker file for the front cover included only the type. A Paper-colored rectangle was drawn over the page number, which had been set on the master pages.

The New England Foundation for the Arts connects the people of New England with the power of art to shape our lives and improve our communities. The Foundation links the public and private sectors in a regional partnership to support and strengthen the arts in the six New England

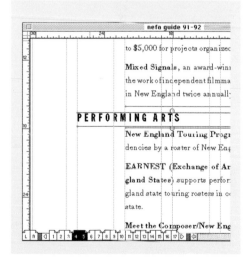

3 Specifying type

For the first issue of the "Guide," Klaetke used Bodoni type set with open leading for "color" and readability — for example, a specification of 9/12 was used for narrow columns, 9.5/14 for text in columns the width of half a page, and 16/24 for a large introductory paragraph, as shown here. Headings were set in Franklin Gothic Extra Condensed in all caps.

4 Setting subheads

To make the subheads for the "Contents" page, rather than set a negative paragraph indent, Klaetke took advantage of the multicolumn grid to set "outdents." He set the subheads and the text as separate text blocks, aligning the left edge of each block with a column guide.

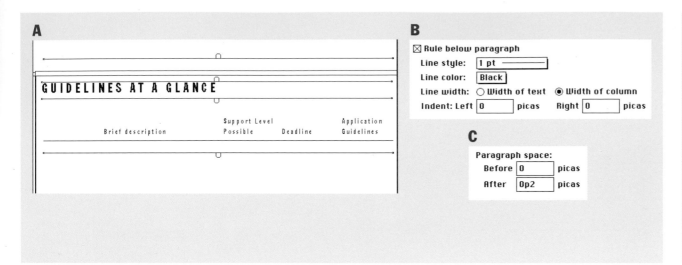

A

GUIDELINES AT A GLANCE

	Support Level		Application
Brief description	Possible	Deadline	Guidelines

B

☒ Rule below paragraph
Line style: `1 pt` ─────
Line color: `Black`
Line width: ○ Width of text ● Width of column
Indent: Left `0` picas Right `0` picas

C

Paragraph space:
Before `0` picas
After `0p2` picas

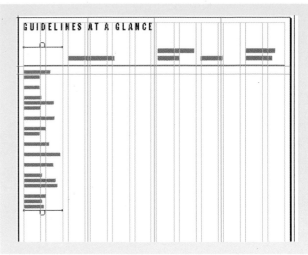

GUIDELINES AT A GLANCE

5 Setting tabular material

The "Guidelines at a Glance" page, which presented funding criteria for various kinds of projects, was set up as a table. Klaetke started by setting the title and the table's column headings as separate blocks (A). To put a 1-point rule below the headings that would span the entire table, he added Space After the paragraph (B) and then specified a Rule Below (C), which PageMaker drew at the bottom of the Space After.

6 Setting the row headings

Klaetke decided not to try to use tabs to set the text for the table, since many of the entries would turn over to additional lines. Instead he set each column, starting with the row headings, as a separate text block. All paragraph styles included 12-point leading. He chose picas for his ruler settings and aligned the first line of text with a pica mark.

7 Completing the text entry

Klaetke typed each block of text, skipping 2 lines between each row entry, and ignoring the need to line up the entries from column to column.

8 Aligning the text to the ruler

Klaetke dragged a horizontal guide to line up with a pica mark on the vertical ruler. By using this guide to align the first line of text in each column, he ensured that baselines would match from column to column and that each line of 9/12 text would fall at a pica mark.

9 Adding space to align the entries

Next he proceeded down the chart row by row, choosing the entry with the most lines and adding Returns in the other columns, so that in the end, all the entries for each row aligned across the chart. He added hairline rules between entries.

10 Finishing the page

For the first issue of the "Guide," Klaetke had pages output at medium-resolution on resin-coated paper. He pasted up mechanical boards, and the printer stripped in photos, as shown here. For the second issue, he output negative film, still leaving the stripping to the printer.

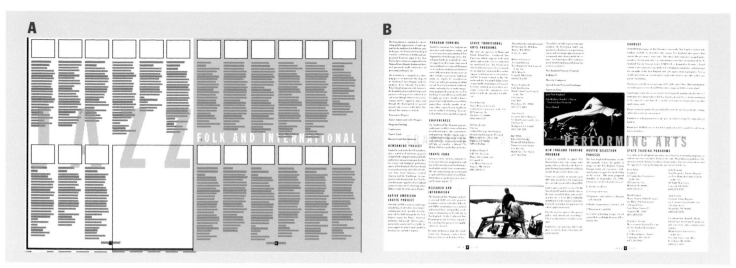

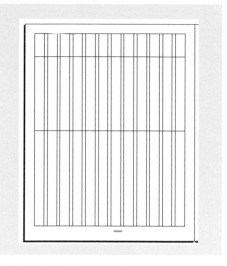

11 Making the most of 2 colors

Both issues of the "Guide" were 2-color printing jobs. Klaetke set up his PageMaker files to show the type that would appear in color and which elements would overprint others (A). He used keylines to designate where the photos would be placed; the color of the keyline indicated whether the photo would print in black or in color, and bleeds were indicated by keylines that extended beyond the edge of the page . Most of the keylines were stripped out by the printer, but those for the small photos were retained to help organize the page. Klaetke used PageMaker's spot color separation option to output the file. But he created the impression of more colors in the first issue by printing the cover on colored stock and by printing 1 of the 16-page signatures (pages 1–8 and 25–32) in gold and black and the other signature (pages 9–24) in green and black (B).

12 Planning photo layouts

To assemble comps for client approval and dummies for the printer, Klaetke needed to paste up copies of the photos. To guide him in sizing, cropping, and applying color treatments, he made a laser-printable grid by snapping 1-point black rules to the column guides.

13 Applying color to the photos

Klaetke layered photos and colors in both issues of the "Guide": Some photos were reproduced in black-and-white (A). Others were printed by substituting a color for black in all (B) or part (C) of the image. A third treatment was to layer a screen of color over a black-and-white image or part of an image (D), and a fourth was a traditional duotone (E). All photo treatment for the first 2 issues was done with traditional prepress methods, but a third issue of the "Guide" will be produced entirely electronically. Here are some examples of how similar photo treatments could be accomplished in PageMaker. For (A) grayscale TIFFs could be imported, assigned the default Black color, and their contrast and brightness adjusted with Image Control. To print an image in color as in (B), the imported grayscale TIFF could be assigned a color through the Colors palette. For (C), 2 copies of the TIFF could be imported, cropped, and assigned colors. For (D) the TIFF could be assigned a tint of black and then overlaid with a large rectangle filled with a 20% tint of color, with Overprint selected in the Fill And Line dialog box; then a smaller version of the TIFF could be placed on top and assigned the default Black. A duotone, like (E), could be created as described in Chapter 42, "Making a Duotone."

Ganging Small Documents

Cher Threinen

To save money on printing, small documents such as business cards can be "ganged" on a single, standard-size sheet. PageMaker's Multiple Paste command helps with the step-and-repeat process used to position several copies of the small document.

1 Designing the logo

Designer Cher Threinen began the job of producing business cards for a Southern California seafood restaurant by designing a logo in Aldus FreeHand. The printer had requested that the final artwork for the business cards be delivered as black-and-white keylines. But Threinen used color in the original artwork for comping purposes.

3 Standardizing on-screen color

Threinen added a type block in Futura Condensed (to match "Fish Market"). Because the screen representation of the green looked like 2 different colors, 1 in the imported EPS file and 1 for items created in PageMaker (A), Threinen changed the color to Pantone 308 CV both in the FreeHand file and in Page-Maker to get consistent color before the client viewed the card on screen (B).

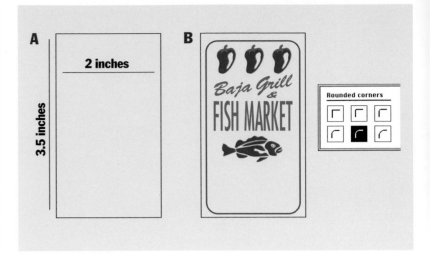

2 Designing the card

To make a color comp for the business card design, Threinen opened a file in PageMaker and drew a 2 x 3.5-inch rectangle to define the shape of the standard-size card (A). She finds that it is often easier for the client to picture the printed card clearly if the edges are defined with an outline rather than with crop marks. Then she placed the FreeHand artwork, which had been saved as an EPS file, and added a rounded-rectangle border (B).

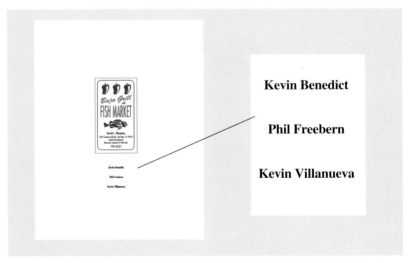

4 Printing a comp

A desktop color print was made for review by the client. In addition to the card design, Threinen included the names of others for whom cards would be made so the client could check and approve the spelling. After approval, Threinen used Save As to create a new copy of the PageMaker business card file. That way she could preserve the color comp file and use the new copy to produce the black-and-white output requested by the printer.

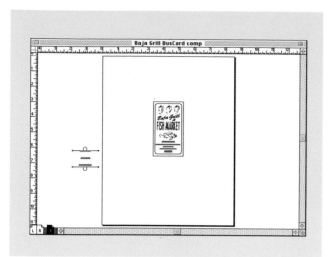

5 Starting the black-and-white layout

Threinen went back to her FreeHand file once again, saved it under a new file name, and changed lines and type to black and fills to None; she exported the file in EPS format. In her new PageMaker file she chose Element, Link Info and linked the new FreeHand EPS in place of the original color file. She recolored the PageMaker type and moved the extra names to the pasteboard.

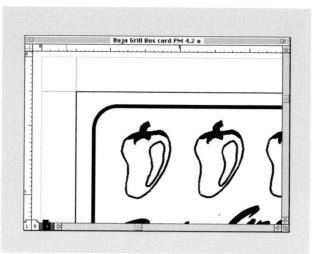

6 Positioning the first card

To save money, Threinen wanted to set up 12 business cards on a single 8.5 x 11-inch sheet. PageMaker's Multiple Paste command would make it easy. Working at 400% view, she began by dragging the zero point of the rulers to the upper left corner of the page. She dragged guidelines to define the corner of the card, and then selected and positioned the artwork.

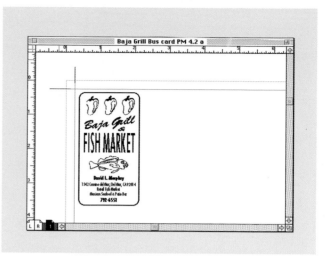

7 Removing the outline

After she had used the Guides and Snap To Guides options to snap the corner of the rectangular card outline into place, Threinen selected and deleted the outline, which she did not want to print. Before deleting the rectangle, however, she used the line tool to add crop marks at the upper left corner of the business card.

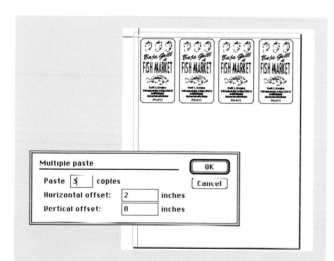

8 Replicating the card

To make a row of 4 cards, Threinen selected all the elements of the card, copied it to the clipboard, and then chose Multiple Paste from the Edit menu. She specified 3 copies in the Multiple Paste dialog box, with a horizontal offset of 2 inches and no vertical offset. This produced a row of cards across the top of the page.

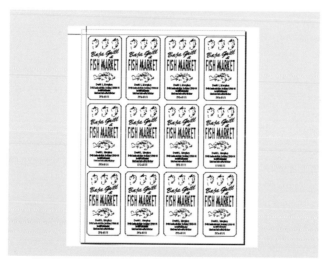

9 Replicating the row

To make 3 rows of cards, Threinen selected all the elements in the top row, copied it to the clipboard, and then chose Multiple Paste from the Edit menu. She specified 2 copies in the Multiple Paste dialog box, with a vertical offset of 3.5 inches and no horizontal offset.

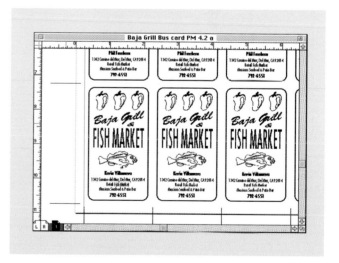

10 Completing the layout

Rather than typing the other names, Threinen used the text tool to select and copy each of the names she had left on the pasteboard and then used the text tool to select and replace the names on some of the cards in the layout. This method ensured that the client-approved spelling of the names would not be accidentally changed. Crop marks were Multiple-Pasted into place.

When birds do sing, hey ding a ding, ding
Sweet lovers love the spring. 🐝 🐝 🐝 🐝

If your PageMaker pages will be printed with an offset printing process, your printer may want you to provide trapping. This chapter explains what trapping is and how it can be achieved in PageMaker. Ask your printer for advice on whether and how much to trap.

Knocking out

PageMaker, like other PostScript-based page design and layout programs, builds pages in layers. When a PageMaker document is printed, colors in lower layers are knocked out so that the colors of objects on upper layers can print clearly.

Preventing gaps

Trapping is the process of building slight overlaps between objects of different colors, so that stretching or shifts can occur during printing without producing gaps.

misregistration   **proper registration**

Understanding misregistration

When a document is printed with more than a single ink color, if the paper stretches or shifts as the sheet moves through the press, *misregistration* can occur. Misregistration of the ink colors can cause gaps so that the unprinted paper of the knock-out shows through. This can be distracting, interfering with the design objective for the page.

too little trap   **too much trap**

Deciding how much trap is needed

With too little trap, gaps can still occur. Too much trap produces an outline or border effect that can be almost as distracting as a gap. The person who will print your pages will know best how much trap will be required for the press conditions, and whether or not you should take responsibility for trapping your PageMaker files. Sometimes no trapping is needed, especially if small sheets are being printed and if the page has been fully assembled in PageMaker.

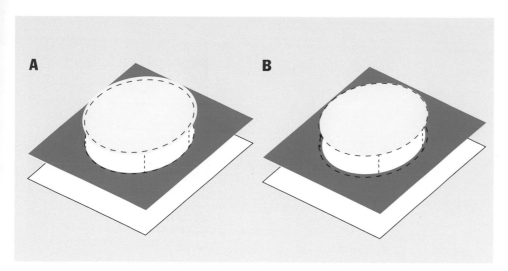

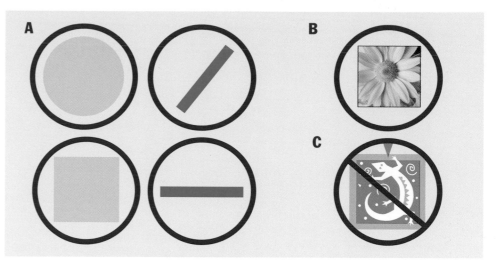

Trapping an element

An object can be trapped either by enlarging the element slightly, called *spreading* (A), or by shrinking the knock-out a little, called *choking* (B). **Note:** All diagrams of trapping in this chapter are exaggerated to make it easier to see the point of the illustrations; in re-

ality, trapping involves extremely narrow overlaps, typically fractions of a point. Other than the exaggerated traps in the diagrams, the art in the chapter has no trap at all, except black overprinting (see page 122).

Understanding what can be trapped in PageMaker

In PageMaker you can trap shapes and lines drawn with the program's own drawing tools (A). And you can create a keyline to trap a rectangular imported image (B). But PageMaker will not trap color within imported graphics (C). For these graphics, trapping must be done in the program of origin, or the entire page may be trapped with specialized software such as Aldus TrapWise when film is produced. Check with your printer or imagesetting service about how pages should be trapped.

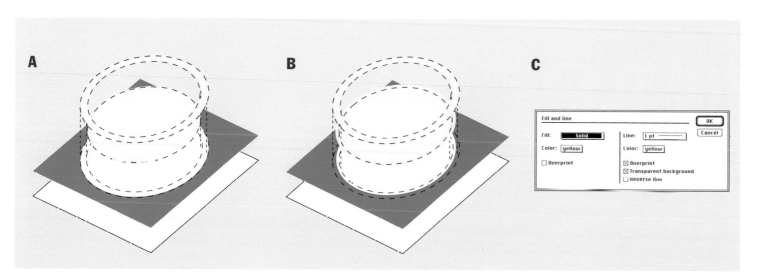

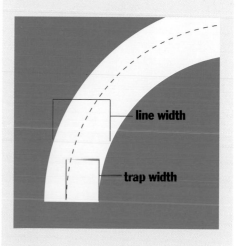

Trapping a shape by overprinting its Line

For rectangles and ovals drawn in PageMaker, the characteristics for *Line* and *Fill* can be specified separately. When the line is not set to Overprint, it extends inward from the edge of the shape, and then the fill starts where the line stops; the knock-out is the full size of the line

and the fill (A). Trapping is done by setting the line to Overprint, which means that the line does not knock out the background color underneath (B); in this case the fill and its knock-out expand outward so that the line partially overlaps the knock-out created by the fill. Overprinting can be set in the Fill And Line dialog box for a

single element (C), or in the Edit Color dialog box for overprinting a particular color anywhere it occurs in the document.

Choosing the right line width

An overprinted line to be used for trapping a shape should be twice the width of the trap, since only half the line will overlap the knock-out.

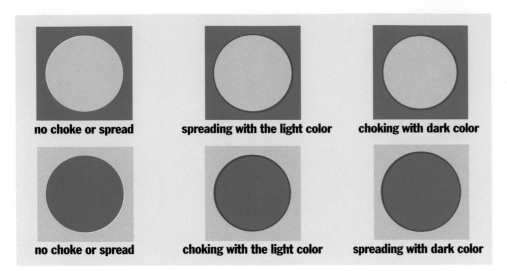

no choke or spread | spreading with the light color | choking with dark color

no choke or spread | choking with the light color | spreading with dark color

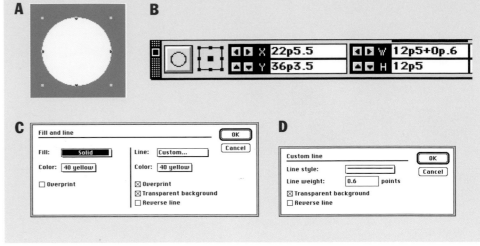

Deciding whether to spread or choke

The decision about whether to spread the object or choke the background depends on the 2 colors involved. To maintain the shape of the object, choke or spread with the lighter color, because the overlap will be less apparent than if you overprint the darker. ● *Ask your printer for advice about trapping very light colors and about other unusual trapping situations.*

Spreading a PageMaker-drawn shape

To spread a shape, increase its size with the Control palette and overprint its Line: Select the object (A) and then select the center button in the proxy box of the Control palette (B). Increase the "H" and "W" values by adding 2 times the trap width. (You double the trap because half the increase will be added to each side of the shape. Rather than doing the addition yourself, you can type "+" and the value; for instance, "+0p0.6" for a 0.3-point trap.) In the Fill And Line dialog box choose Custom (C), set the Line to overprint, and make a Line the same color as the Fill. Use 2 times the trap for the Line weight (D).

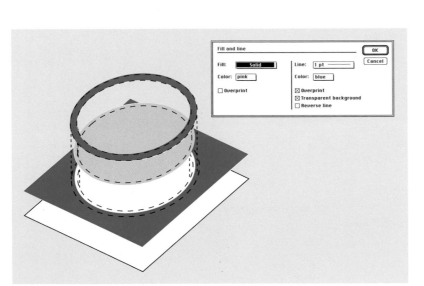

Choking a PageMaker-drawn shape

Choking can be done simply by adding a stroke that is the same color as the background and twice the width of the trap, and designating it to overprint in the Fill And Line dialog box.

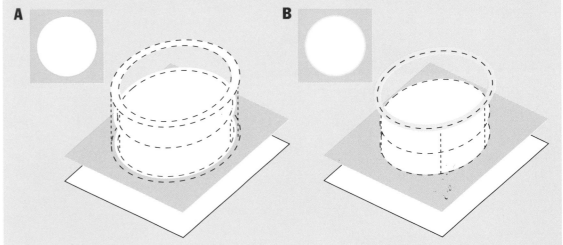

Trapping with a third color

Sometimes the color that forms from the overlap when a trapping stroke is added to a pale object on a pale background is markedly darker than either of the 2 original colors, producing an outline effect (A). In that case, you can overprint a stroke that is a lighter tint of the mix of the 2 colors (B). ● *When a color overprints another, the printed color that results is a mix of the components of the top (overprinting) color and any additional components of the bottom color. For example, if the top color is 20C, 30M, 10Y and the bottom color is 40C, 20M, 10K, the result will be 20C, 30M, 10Y, 10K.*

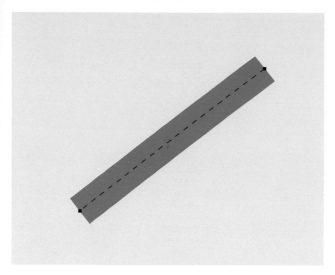

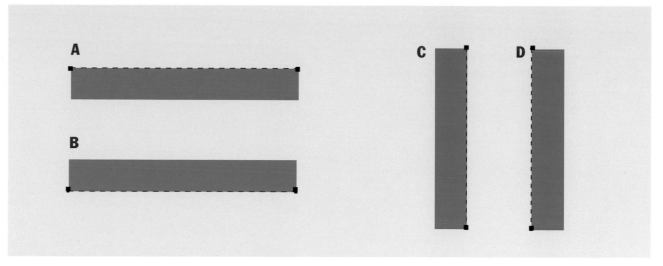

Constructing slanted lines in PageMaker

To understand how to trap a line in PageMaker, you have to understand how the program constructs lines. Slanted lines are easy to understand: As in many other PostScript programs, the path that determines the line is in the center of the line, and half the thickness of the line goes to each side.

Constructing vertical and horizontal lines in PageMaker

The thickness of a horizontal or vertical line extends from one edge instead of going both ways from the center. The direction it extends depends on how you drag the cursor as you draw the line. If you drag down slightly as you draw a horizontal line, it extends down from its top edge (A); drag up to extend it from its bottom edge (B). Dragging left or right determines how a vertical line is drawn (C, D).

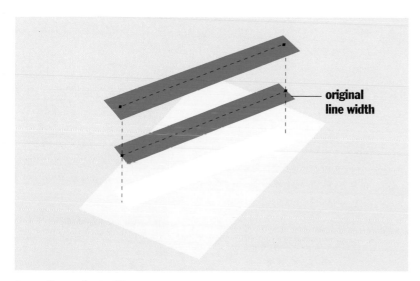

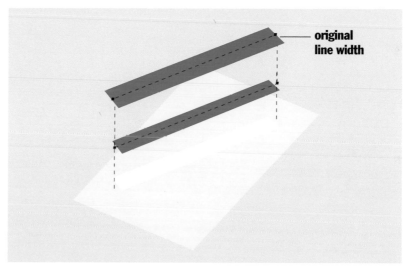

Spreading a slanted line

To spread a slanted line, select it, copy it, and use Option-Paste to put the copy exactly on top of the original. In the Fill And Line dialog box, add 2 times the trap to the Line width. The added thickness will spread from the center, creating the proper trap at each edge of the line. Set this top line to Overprint. In the Control palette, select the center point in the proxy and add 2 times the trap to the "L" (length) value. The overprinted line, thicker than the knock-out, creates the trap.

Choking a slanted line

To choke a slanted line, select it and copy it to the clipboard. With the original line still selected, make it thinner by subtracting 2 times the trap (in the Fill And Line dialog box); the line will shrink inward toward the center. In the Control palette choose the center point in the proxy box and then decrease "L" (the length) by 2 times the trap value. Now Option-Paste the copy of the from the clipboard, and set this line to Overprint in the Fill and Line dialog box.

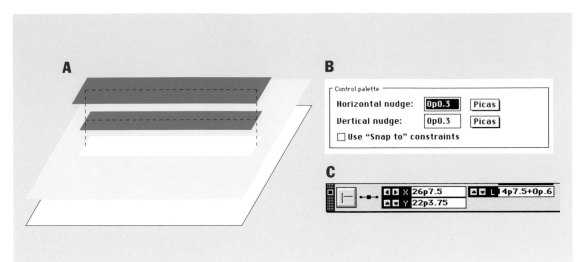

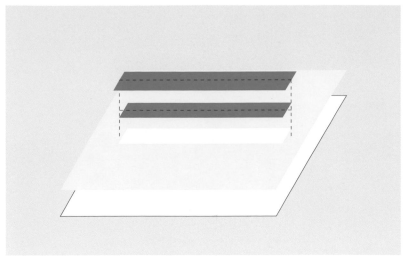

Spreading a horizontal or vertical line

To spread a horizontal or vertical line (A), make a fatter version by copying, Option-Pasting, increasing the line width, and designating it to Overprint. Under Edit, Preferences, set the Nudge distance to be the same as the trap (B). Then use the nudge buttons in the Control palette to move this fatter copy up, down, left, or right by the trap amount so it overlaps both edges of the line (C). Also, select the center point of the proxy and increase the "L" (length) setting by 2 times the trap amount.

Choking a horizontal or vertical line

First copy the line to the clipboard. Decrease the weight of the original line by 2 times the trap you want. Choose the center point in the proxy box and decrease the "L" measurement by twice the trap value. Under Edit, Preferences, set the Nudge distance to be the same as the trap you want. Use the nudge buttons in the Control palette to move this original line up, down, left, or right by the trap amount. Option-Paste the line stored in the clipboard and set it to Overprint.

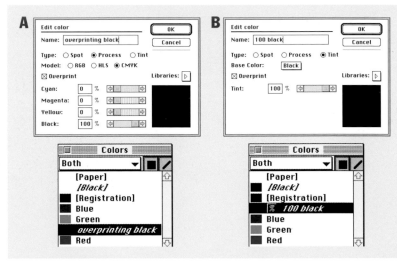

Understanding how PageMaker treats black

Since black is dark enough to cover other colors, it can be trapped by overprinting it on top of other colors. By default, PageMaker 5.0's Black *does not* overprint. That is, if you draw a black rectangle, oval, or line, or if you import a TIFF image, it will knock out colors beneath it (A). There is one exception to this black default knock-out rule, however: Black type automatically overprints (B).

Overprinting black

To give yourself 2 options — a black that overprints and a black that does not overprint — so you can get 100% black to overprint not only for text but elsewhere in the document, Command-click Black in the Color palette to open the Edit Color dialog box and then define a process black and choose Overprint (A). Or use Define Colors to create a 100% Tint of black to overprint (B). Assign your new color or tint to any elements that you want to overprint in black.

Avoiding the need for trapping process colors

For an illustration prepared with process printing colors (cyan, magenta, yellow, and black), color separation results in a printing plate for each of these primary colors (A). These plates are used to apply the inks on top of each other. Because of the way the colors are printed, 1 way to avoid the potential for white gaps due to misregistration is to make sure that every color you use in a layout shares at least 1 primary color component with every other color in the layout (B).

That way, when separations are made, every area of color on the page is covered by at least 2 inks. If misregistration occurs when the illustration is printed, a sliver of the shared color will shown, but this is usually much less distracting than white would be. Ask your printer for advice on the percentage of shared color to use.

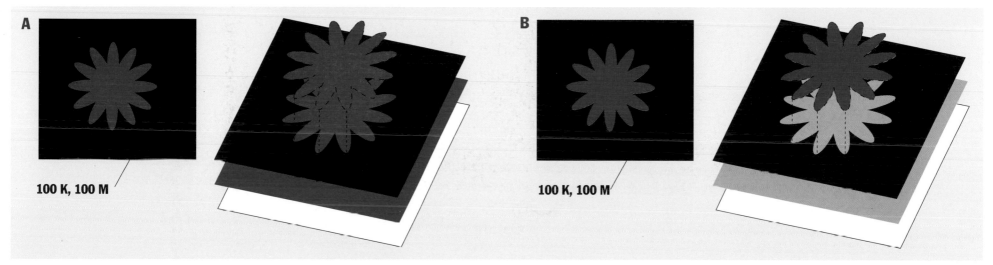

Trapping color against black

When you want to trap a colored shape or type against a black background, you can add the color to the black. This is equivalent to adding a layer (or layers) of color under the black (A). It not only provides trap but also makes the black richer, as you can see by comparing the three black swatches shown here (B). Check with your printer to make sure that this procedure will not result in a total ink coverage that is too much to print well. If necessary, reduce the percentage of color.

Overprinting a black-and-white TIFF

An imported 1-bit TIFF is black by default when it is placed on a PageMaker page. Therefore, by default it will knock out of colors beneath it (A). Since the Fill And Line dialog box is not available for assigning color to an imported TIFF, there is no way to assign object-level overprinting. So the only way to get the black part of an imported TIFF image to overprint a color underneath it is to assign it a color that universally overprints, as set in the Define Colors dialog box (B).

Trapping a TIFF with a keyline

One way to trap an imported image on a white page is to overprint a keyline. Select the TIFF and choose Create Keyline from the Aldus Additions submenu under Utilities. Enter a zero in the Extend box of the Create Keyline dialog box, and select Bring Keyline To Front. Choose Knock Out Under Keyline and enter the trap width in the Overlap box. Click Attributes, and in the Fill And Line dialog box choose Line color and weight, and choose overprint. For Fill, choose None.

Trapping a black-and-white or grayscale TIFF against color

To trap a monochrome or grayscale image against background color, you can put a slightly smaller knock-out behind it and color the image to overprint: Select the TIFF and choose Create Keyline from Utilities, Aldus Additions. Enter the trap value as a negative number in the Extend box, select Send Keyline Behind, and click Attributes to open Fill And Line. Choose a Solid Fill in Paper Color. Select the TIFF and assign it a color that has been set to overprint.

50

Producing a Book: 1

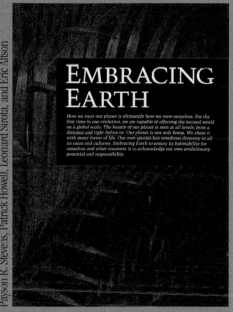

Payson R. Stevens, Patrick Howell, Leonard Sirota, and Eric Altson

When InterNetwork, Inc. undertook to produce the book *Embracing Earth: New Views of Our Changing Planet* for Chronicle Books, the entire project — from idea to printed books — had to be completed in 6 months. The design firm, whose president, Payson R. Stevens, co-authored the book, intertwined the writing, design, and production processes.

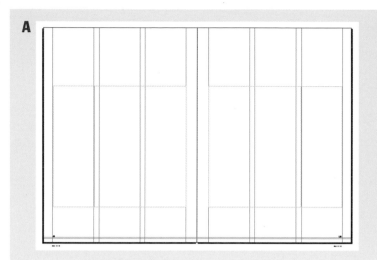

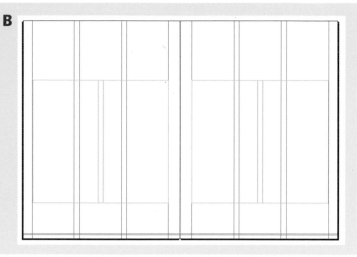

1 Designing 2 kinds of pages

InterNetwork's goal was to develop the large-format (10 x 14-inch) *Embracing Earth* as a portrait of the planet, both its natural rhythms and human impact upon it, as seen from space. The design began with master pages set up with 3 columns on each page. Guidelines extended the column boundaries into the wide top and bottom margins. For most pages of the book, Copy Master Guides was chosen, so that this layout would serve as a guide for flowing text and placing photos (A). Because the pages were set up as Double-Sided, Facing Pages, side margins could be set as Inside and Outside; the inside margins were slightly wider. For the Preface and the introductory pages of the book's 4 sections, Column Guides was used to set up a 2-column grid (B). As the 176-page book developed, files were organized into 10-page sections (10–19, 20–29, and so on) for ease of handling.

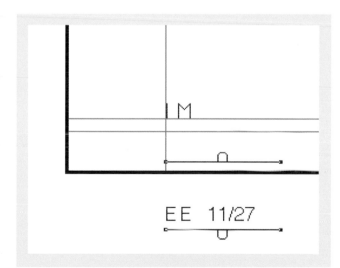

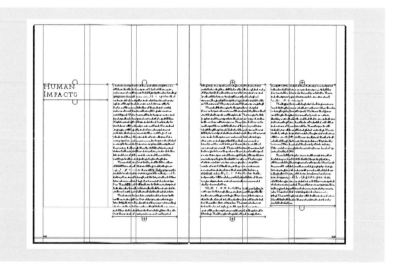

2 Keeping track of versions of the layout

PageMaker updates the "Last Modified" date of a file whenever any change is made — even a relatively trivial change such as the page range printed or the page at which the file opens. So the designers created "date tags," independent text blocks on the master pages that extended onto the pasteboard. They updated the tags to keep track of their various versions of the layout.

3 Placing text

As the book progressed, the text, which author/designer Payson R. Stevens wrote over each weekend, was placed in PageMaker files the following week. Text was placed with the Autoflow feature turned on so that it flowed from column to column automatically. The designers then adjusted the column lengths, sometimes editing text to fit. The margins that had been established on the master pages served as guides but were not strictly adhered to.

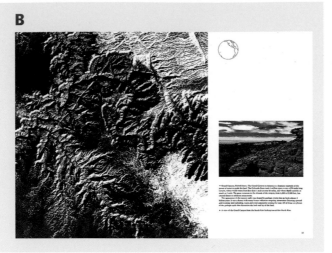

A

⌖ Grand Canyon, United States. T
power of water to erode the land. T
canyon, whose width varies from le
much as 1 mile. The great variation
created desert to subarctic ecosyste

The appearance of the canyon w
billion years. It was a drama with r
and twisting, land subsiding, water
of the geologic cycle that determin

⌖ A view of the Grand Canyon fro

B

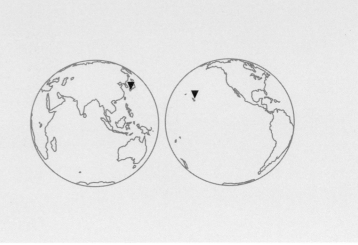

4 Captioning the photos

Photos and data graphics for the book were scanned at low resolution (72 dpi) in color to be used as placeholders in the layouts as the book developed. Much of the text in the book was presented as captions for the images. On spreads with more than 1 image, designers used arrows imported as Aldus FreeHand EPS files to point from caption to image (A). Photos that occupied a full spread were captioned on the next page, with 2 arrows to indicate that the photo was on the overleaf (B).

5 Importing maps for orientation

To pinpoint the region of the earth's surface shown in each image, the designers used a line-art representation of the globe at the top of the page (see step 4), keyed with an arrow. For spreads showing more than one location, the arrows would be color-keyed when printed. The globes were made with a public domain program such as Earthplot, which generates a bitmap or PICT map from a user-specified longitude, latitude, and altitude; these maps were then traced in FreeHand.

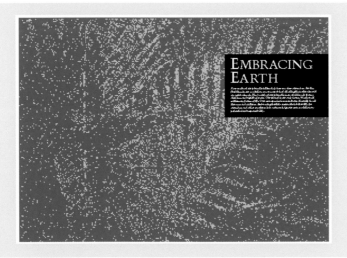

6 Creating mezzotints

Each of the four sections of the book opened with a title spread, with type reversed out of a black rectangle that was placed on top of a photo. The photo had been sized and given a mezzotint look by converting it to a low-resolution black-and-white bitmap in Adobe Photoshop, using the Diffusion Dither. It was placed on the page, and the black rectangle was added. Type was set on a separate page.

7 Tracking progress with thumbnails

To track the relationship of text and graphics and the flow of material throughout the book, designers made 8-to-a-page Thumbnail prints (set in the Print Document dialog box) on a desktop color printer. Printing color thumbnail pages for the entire book was also a cost-efficient way to show the publisher how the project was developing.

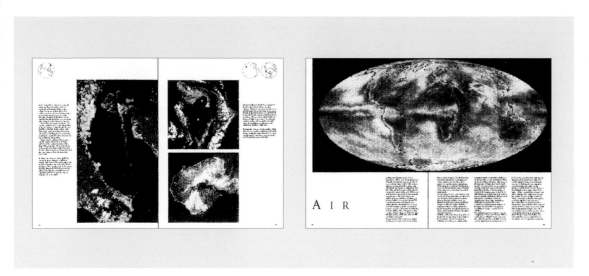

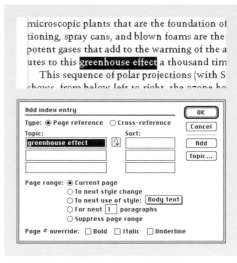

8 Rearranging spreads

The book is organized largely in spreads of photos and their captions, and there were many possible ways to order the presentation of information. To be able to experiment with the order of spreads, the InterNetwork designers made "spread cards" (shown here at full size) by cutting the thumbnail prints and gluing them onto card stock. This way they could lay the cards out on a table to experiment with the pacing of the book. After spreads had been rearranged, new color thumbnail prints could be made. 🍎 *PageMaker 5 allows you to open several layout files at once and to drag text blocks and graphics between files.* 🍎 *The Sort Pages Addition lets you change the order of pages in a file.*

9 Building an index

The InterNetwork team compiled an index for the book. 🍎 *To use PageMaker's indexing function, select a word with the text tool and choose Options, Index Entry (or use Command-semicolon). You can also use the command to type entries and subentries. Use the Format command from the Create Index dialog box to determine whether alphabetic headings will be included in the index listing (as shown here) and whether subentries will be run in..*

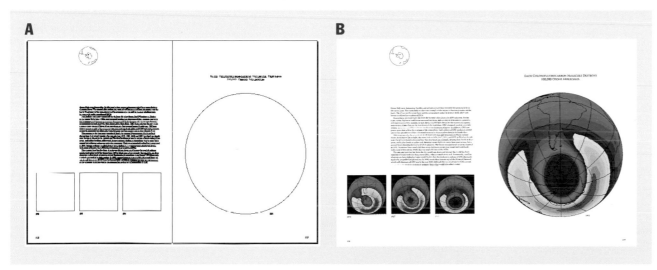

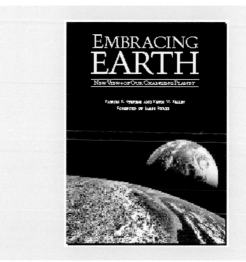

10 Drawing keylines

When the layouts for the book were complete and had been approved by the publisher, the InterNetwork designers replaced the photos that had been used for position only with nonprinting keylines. Marked laser prints indicated to the printer which image would go in each box. Once the keylines had been drawn, the place-holders for the photos were removed (A). Pages were output at medium resolution on resin-coated paper, and photos were color-separated and stripped in. Computer-generated graphics were output as film transparencies (B). 🍎 *To make a keyline that exactly fits a photo or other imported graphic, use the Create Keyline Aldus Addition: Choose Utilities, Additions, Create Keyline; then click on the button to bring the keyline in front of the object so that the keyline will overprint its edges.*

11 Designing cover studies

The designers were asked to develop several options for the jacket of the book. One of their cover studies included a photo-montage of two views of earth, which the designers created in Adobe Photoshop and placed in the PageMaker file.

51

Producing a Book: 2

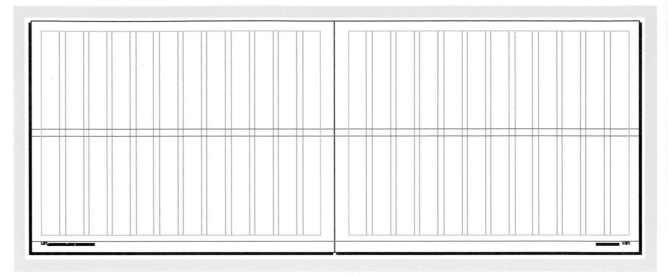

Aldus PageMaker
A Visual Guide for the Mac

A step-by-step approach to learning page layout software

Linnea Dayton and Janet Ashford

This book was designed and produced in Aldus PageMaker. The next 5 pages tell how it was done.

1 Creating master pages

The book you are holding, *Aldus PageMaker: A Visual Guide for the Mac*, was created with PageMaker. It includes graphics in a variety of sizes and formats. In planning the book we knew we would need a page design that was flexible but still orderly. Within the framework of the 8.5 x 11-inch horizontal-format book, we developed a 12-column underlying grid on the master pages so that figures could vary in width from 2 to 12 columns. Horizontal guidelines help in the placement of captions, keeping free a 0.25-inch horizontal gutter in the center of each page. Master pages also include running feet with the book title, chapter title, and page numbers.

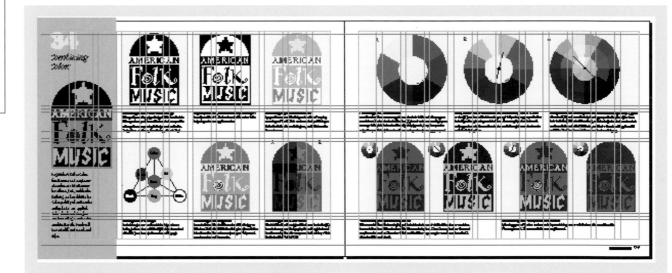

2 Using 3-column figures

All the chapters begin with a 3-column-wide gray band that bleeds off the top, bottom, and left side of the opening page and provides a framework for holding the chapter number, title, opening figure, and a brief synopsis. The simplest layout consists of figure frames that are 3 columns wide, with the grid making it possible to fit 4 of these across a page. For a very wide figure all 12 columns can be used. Each figure frame is separated from the caption below it by 0.125 inches.

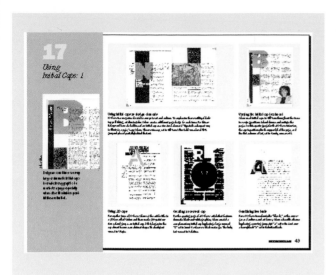

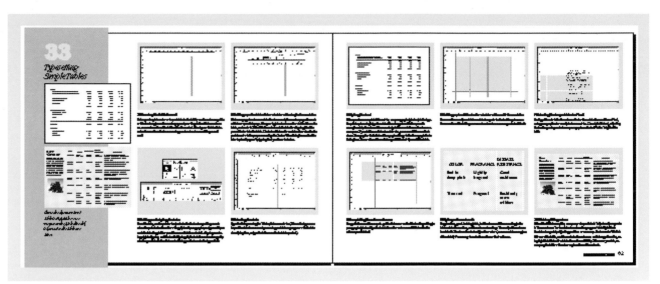

3 Doubling the 3-column size

An obvious extension of the 3-column figure size for artwork that is quite a bit wider than it is long is to use a 6-column figure space. This shape is easy to combine on what is basically a 3-column spread.

4 Using 4-column figures

Sometimes the opening figure is sized to a 4-column width so that it extends beyond the gray band. In these cases, the rest of the figures on the opening page must fit within 8 columns, usually in figure frames that are 4 columns wide.

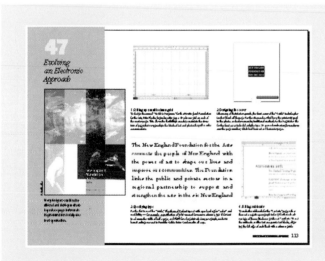

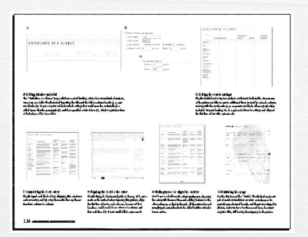

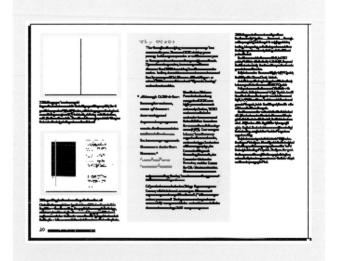

5 Combining figure widths

We used a 4-column-wide format to show detail in the opening figure for this spread. The first 2 figures on the page are also 4 columns wide, but the third and fourth are 5 and 3 columns wide respectively, in order to accommodate the different formats of the graphics. On the following page it worked best to size the figure frames in units of 8 and 4 at the top and units of 3 at the bottom. Figure frames were fitted to the grid simply by dragging their corner handles from one guideline to the next. *The Snap To Guides function ensures that text blocks and figures are aligned to the grid by pulling these elements tight against the nearest guideline.*

6 Creating a flexible layout

Some pages of the book required a more flexible layout. To accommodate large vertical figures on this page, the first 2 figures, which are horizontal, are 4 columns wide and are positioned 1 above the other.

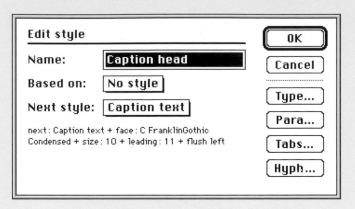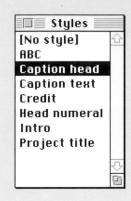

7 Designing the chapter opener

We wanted a neutral color for the vertical band that signals a new chapter, to serve as a background for the artwork. Black offered a striking contrast but seemed too "heavy." We chose a gray composed of 40% each cyan magenta, and yellow, which eliminated the need for trap (see page 118, "Trapping.")

8 Styling type

Type for the captions is set in Garamond Condensed Light (chosen for its compactness since text space was limited) at 10/11 points with Tight track. The sanserif Franklin Gothic Condensed used for the heading provides good contrast. The Caption Head style was defined with Caption Text as the Next

Style, so that pressing Return at the end of the heading would automatically start a paragraph with the appropriate style. Five more styles were defined: Head Numeral, 60-point Franklin Gothic Heavy bold in a 20% CMY gray; Project Title, 26/24 Garamond Light Condensed italic; Intro, Garamond Condensed Light at 12/Auto with Tight track; Credit, like Intro but 10 points.

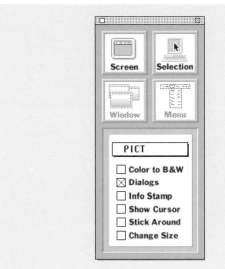

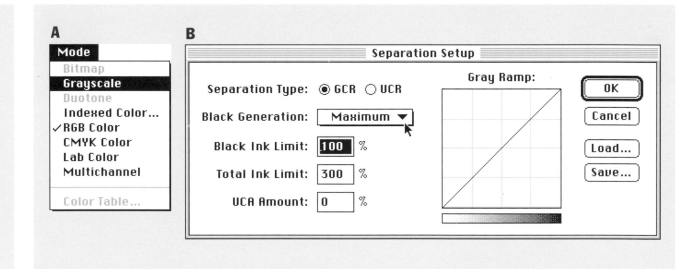

9 Making screen captures

Many of the illustrations in the book show files as they appear on screen. To capture these views, we used Screenshot, a Control Panel utility. By pressing a key (F1 by default) we could take a snapshot of a window, menu, or selected area; we could name it and save it as a PICT file.

10 Converting PICTs to TIFFs

Since PICT files do not separate well for printing, we used Adobe Photoshop to convert the screen shots to TIFF format, and edited them as needed. We knew the book would be translated into several languages, with dialog boxes to match. To make it as easy as possible to replace the black parts of the dia-

log boxes, we converted all dialog boxes that were without color to grayscale TIFFs (A). Dialog boxes that included color were converted to CMYK TIFF format, with Photoshop's Separation Setup set for Maximum Black Generation, so the black elements would contain no cyan, magenta, or yellow (B). That way, the replacement dialog boxes could be stripped into the black plate only.

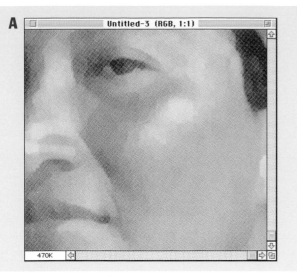

A

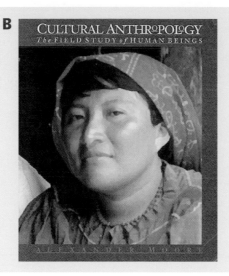

B

11 Importing scans

In addition to screen shots, other artwork, such as final printed pieces, was imported into PageMaker as scans saved as TIFF files. Scans were made on a desktop or a drum scanner so that they would have a resolution of 300 dpi at the final size at which they were printed in this book. In some cases these files showed scanning artifacts such as blurring or moiré (an interference pattern caused by the interaction of the scanning pattern and the pattern of dots of ink that had been used to print the piece) (A). These artifacts were removed by applying Adobe Photoshop's Despeckle filter to remove unwanted fine-scale patterns and applying the Unsharp Mask filter to sharpen the image (B).

12 Importing EPS artwork files

Art files that had been prepared on the computer as components of projects shown in the book were imported into PageMaker in EPS (encapsulated PostScript) or TIFF format. EPS was used for Adobe Illustrator and Aldus FreeHand files.

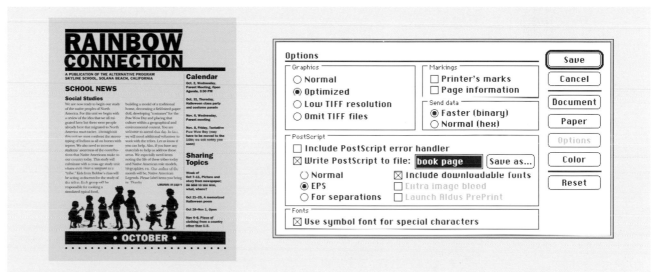

13 Importing TIFF images

TIFF (or tagged image file format) was used for photos and for artwork generated in Adobe Photoshop and other color bitmap programs. ⌘ *PageMaker 5, by itself, can produce color separations from CMYK TIFFs; Aldus PrePrint can separate RGB TIFFs in PageMaker files.*

14 Making EPSs of PageMaker pages

To show intermediate stages of page layout projects or to show the final layouts for projects that were prepared entirely electronically, we either made screen captures on a 19-inch monitor or made EPS files though PageMaker's Print command: We chose File, Print to open the Print dialog box, entered the number of the page we wanted to save in EPS form, and then pressed the Options button and chose Write PostScript To File, selecting the EPS option; we named the file and pressed the Save button to make the EPS file. Then the file could be placed on our book page like other EPSs.

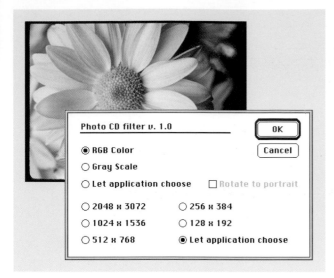

histogram

15 Importing Kodak Photo CD images

Some of the photo images, such as the one in the "Trapping" chapter were in Kodak Photo CD format, a file format used for storing photos from film on compact disc in several resolutions. ● *PageMaker 5 can import Photo CD files directly through the Place command.*

16 Labeling artwork

We used the Caption Head style with leader lines to provide the labels for some of the figures; the type was distinctive enough to stand out from any type that might be part of the figure. Because black type overprints by default, the type occurs only on the black plate, again helpful for translations.

17 Using an indicator color

To identify a specific region of a figure, to help you find the part that is being described, we colored a part of the image or used a PageMaker shape, typically a circle, in a red color composed of 100% magenta and yellow, with 10% cyan added in order to avoid the need for trap (see Chapter 49).

18 Making laser prints

To send page proofs to the publisher for proofreading and translation into other languages, we printed our PageMaker files as composite (not color-separated) pages on a LaserWriter Plus and a LaserWriter IINTX. In some cases the number of complex EPS files on the page resulted in very long printing times. To speed up the printing process in these cases, we substituted screen captures (PICTs) for the complex artwork: We chose Actual Size from the Page menu to display our PageMaker files on screen, and then used Screenshot to capture a selection that included the artwork. We selected the original artwork and dragged it off the page, placing the screen capture in its place. Several chapters were printed at once using the Book command, which allows you to print several files, one after the other, without having to enter the Print command for each individual file. After the laser proof was made, the original artwork could be replaced before the file was sent to the imagesetter for separation.

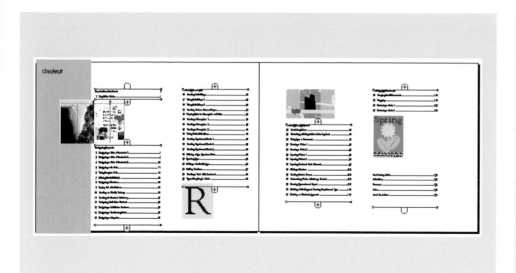

19 Preparing the table of contents

The projects were arranged in the book in 4 categories: designing layouts, working with type, working with graphics, and managing production. Within these groups, chapters were arranged in an order dictated by their complexity and their relationship to other projects in that group. Once the final order had been determined, the table of contents was compiled by hand.

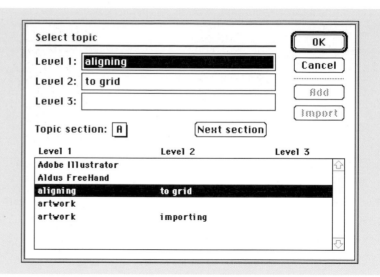

20 Creating the index

In order to make a single index from all the chapters, we compiled a book list of all the chapter files. We began the indexing process by creating a Topics list. After working in the individual chapters to make index entries, we reviewed the entries with Show Index and then used Create Index to compile the index.

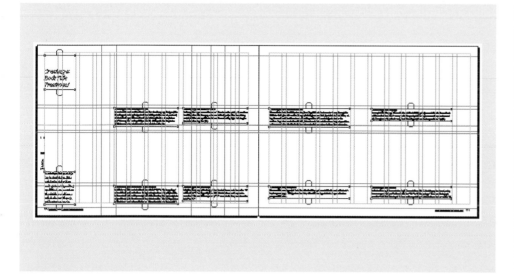

21 Preparing translations

The translators were supplied with our PageMaker layout files so they could fit their translations directly into the caption space provided. To protect contributing artists from having their electronic files circulated, we removed all the original EPS and TIFF files from the layouts.

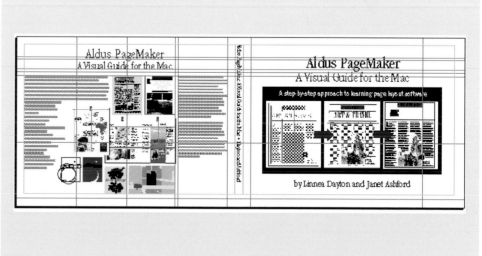

22 Preparing the cover and printing the book

The book's cover was also prepared in PageMaker, using the method described in Chapter 9, "Laying Out a Book Cover." The cover and book chapter files were output as negative film at 150 lines per inch; Matchprints were made to check color. The book's inside pages were printed on 128 gsm Mat Artpaper and the cover on 260 gsm gloss laminated Artboard.

Contributing Artists

Rich Borge
Gravity Workshop
124 Maney Avenue
Asheville, NC 28804
704/251-1795

Calvin Woo Associates
4015 Ibis Street
San Diego, CA 92107
619/299-0431

Diane Fenster
140 Berendos Avenue
Pacifica, CA 94044
415/355-5007

Tom Gould
2966 Dove Street
San Diego, CA 92103
619/298-8605

Leah Hewitt
UCSD Publications
10300 N. Torrey Pines Road
La Jolla, CA 92093-0941
619/534-4754

Hopkins-Baumann
236 W. 26th Street, Suite 5NW
New York, NY 10001
212/727-2929

Hornall Anderson Design Works
1008 Western Avenue, Sixth floor
Seattle, WA 98104
206/467-5800

Fritz Klaetke
Visual Dialogue
429 Columbus Avenue, #1
Boston, MA 02116
617/247-3658

Darlene McElroy
3723 Birch Street, #14
Newport Beach, CA 92660
714/434-7220

John Odam
John Odam Design Associates
2163 Cordero Avenue
Del Mar, CA 92014
619/259-8230

InterNetwork, Inc.
411 7th Street
Del Mar, CA 92014
619/755-0439

Cher Threinen
Cher Threinen Design
485-1/2 San Gorgonio Street
San Diego, CA 92106
619/226-6050

Sigi Torinus
185 Collingwood Street
San Francisco, CA 94114
415/558-8346

Definitions

A listing of acronyms used in this book, what they stand for, and what they mean

DCS (Desktop Color Separation)
A specialized EPS (see below) file format that uses 5 components — 1 each for the cyan, magenta, yellow, and black color separation plates — and 1 composite image for screen display and low-resolution printing

EPS or **EPSF** (Encapsulated PostScript Format)
A PostScript language file that includes a PICT component (see below) so an image can be displayed on screen and the file can be printed from a non-PostScript printer

PS (PostScript)
The page description language that PageMaker and other desktop graphics programs use to generate instructions for output of graphics files

PICT/PICT2
A standard Macintosh format for black-and-white and color graphics

TIFF (Tagged Image File Format)
A file format used for scanned images and other bitmapped graphics

Resources

A listing of the programs, typefaces, and other software resources mentioned in this book. (All typefaces mentioned in the book are from Adobe Systems, Inc. unless otherwise noted.)

Aldus PageMaker 5.0 and **Aldus FreeHand** are available in the United States and Pacific Rim from the Aldus Corporation
411 First Avenue South
Seattle, WA 98104-2871
USA
Tel. 206/622-5500

and in Europe from
Aldus Europe Limited
Aldus House
West One Business Park
5 Mid New Cultins
Edinburgh, Scotland
United Kingdom EH11 4DU
Tel. 44 31 453 2211

Adobe Illustrator, Adobe Streamline, Adobe Photoshop, and **Adobe typefaces** are available in the United States from Adobe System Incorporated
1585 Charleston Road
Mountain View, CA 94039-7900

in Europe from
Adobe Systems Europe B.V.
Europlaza, Hoogoorddreef 54a
1101 BE Amsterdam Z-O
The Netherlands

and in Japan from
Adobe Systems Japan
Swiss Bank House
4-1-8 Toranomon, Minato-ku
Tokyo 105
Japan

BarCode Pro is available from
Synex
692 10th Street
Brooklyn, NY 11215-4502
USA
718-499-6293

DiscImagery stock photo collections are available from
Gazelle Technologies, Inc.
7434 Trade Street
San Diego, CA 92121
USA
619/536-9999

EarthPlot is available from
Educorp
7434 Trade Street
San Diego, CA 92121
USA
619/536-9999

Emigre typefaces are available from
Emigre Graphics
4475 D Street
Sacramento, CA 95819
USA

Flowers and other stock photo titles are available from
Digital Stock
400 S. Sierra Avenue
Solana Beach, CA 92075
USA
619/794-404

Images with Impact clip art is available from
3G Graphics
114 Second Avenue S, Suite 104
Edmonds, WA 98020
USA
206/774-3518

MathType is available from
Design Science
4028 Broadway
Long Beach, CA 90803
USA
310-433-0685

OPTIFonts typefaces are available from
Eagle Graphic Systems
1824 Lakeshore Court
Fort Collins, CO 80525
USA
303-226-4567

Screenshot is available from
Baseline Publishing, Inc.
1770 Moriah Woods Boulevard
Suite 14
Memphis, TN 38117
USA
901/682-9676

Index

A

Additions, Aldus, 3, 7, 44, 77, 78
ads, designing, 31
annual reports, 16-17, 106-109
Autoflow, 14, 125

B

background texture, 48
Baseline Offset, 78
baseline shift, 57
baselines, aligning from column to column, 33
black, overprinting, 97
"blendo," 49
Book command, 7
book covers, designing, 22-23, 127, 133
book production, 125-127, 128-133
book titles, designing, 80-81
borders, 12, 64-65, 2
brochures, designing, 18-21, 32-33, 74-76
Build Booklet Addition, 7
bullets
    square, 21, 42
    used as spacers, 24. 28, 56
business cards, designing, 27, 28, 116-117
bylines, designing, 43

C

calendar template, 3
capitals
    boxed, 48
    drop, 44
    hanging, 45, 46
    imported, 46
    initial, 35, 39, 44, 49, 50, 55, 71, 72
    raised, 44
    reverse, 49
    small, 25
    three-dimensional, 49
captions, designing, 12, 17, 36, 125
catalogs, designing, 69-73, 113-115
chapter opener pages, 81
clip art, 50, 110
color separation, 7
color wheel, 85

color, reversing, 19
colors
    complementary, 85, 86
    two, designing with, 115
column grids, 11-13, 14, 16-17, 113
    underlying, 14, 17, 113
    violating, for effect, 13
    visible, 16-17
column guides, 11, 16, 36, 66
columns
    curved, 52, 53
    custom shapes, 51-53
    triangular, 51
    unequal widths, 11
complements (color), 85
    double complements, 86
    multiple complements, 86
    near complements, 85
    triadic complements, 86
contents, table of (*see* table of contents)
Control palettes, 3, 43, 111
covers, designing, 22-23, 81, 109, 113,127
credit lines, 30
cropping, 6, 78
Custom line width, 95
    defining, 18, 98
    muted tones, 87
    neutral, 87
    pastels, 86, 90
    tones, mixing, 87

D

department heads, creating, 62. 63. 64-65
dingbats, 42, 47, 56, 71, 91
    as paragraph separators, 71, 73
    square, 42, 71
Display Master Items, 26
display of graphics, at Normal or High Resolution, 6
dot screen, 102-103
dotted line, vertical, 106
drawing tools, 60, 111
Drop Cap Addition, 44-45
drop caps, 44, 45, 46
duotones, creating, 100-101

E

Earthplot, 126
envelopes, designing, 25, 28 ,29

F

fills
    color, 18
    pattern, 6
flipping, 60
folding, guides for, 28
folios, 36
font chart, making, 91
for position only (*see* FPO)
Force Justify, 31, 56, 71, 74, 75
FPO scans, 13
Fraction, Aldus Addition, 77
fractions
    adjusting spacing, weights, widths, 79
    as inline graphics, 78
    kerning parts of, 78, 79
    setting, 77-79
framing, 94, 95
function keys, 3

G

ganging small documents, 116-117
golden section, 26
grabber hand, 3, 78
graphics, imported
    display of, at Normal or High resolution, 6
    inline (*see* inline graphics)
    linking, 39
    updating, from within PageMaker, 6
    viewing, 36
graphs, 106-109
grid (*see* also column grid)
grid of fifths, 26
grouping, with PS GroupIt Addition, 60, 78
Guides And Rules, 66
guides, column, 11
guides, horizontal, 30, 71, 74, 83
guides, vertical, 36, 71
gutter, specifying 11

H

halftone screens
    custom, 102-103, 105
    simulated, 103
hanging caps, 45, 46
headlines, 52, 61
histogram, designing, 109
histogram, Image Control (*see* Image Control)
Horizontal Fraction Addition, 79

I

identity package, developing, 24-26
Image Control, 96-97, 100-101, 104-105
inch marks, 5
indents, 20, 33
indexing, 127
initial caps, 35, 39, 44-48, 49, 50, 55, 71, 72
    drawing, 47
    drop, 44, 45
    raised, 44
inline graphics, 5, 38, 108
    fractions as, 78, 79

J

justified type, 31, 56, 71, 74, 75

K

Keep Lines Together, 38
kerning, 57, 59, 78, 79, 80
kerning, positive, 37
keyboard shortcuts, 3
keylines, 16, 127

L

labels, product, 31
layering graphic elements, 2, 96-97, 99
leading
    Auto, 80
    negative, 48, 80
    open, 71, 75, 76
letterhead, 24
letterspacing problems, 38
letterspacing, 56, 59, 70, 72, 92
Library palette, 2
line
    dotted, custom, 106
    transparent background, 6
line screen 102-103, 105
line tool, used for illustrating, 60
line width, Custom, 94, 95
linking graphics files, 5, 9
low-resolution photos as placeholders, 38

M

magazines, designing, 34-39, 40-43, 63
magnifying view, 3
mail-order products, 30-31
mailing labels, designing, 25, 29, 30
maps, creating, 126
margins, specifying 11

masking, with Paper-color shapes, 90
master guides, copying, 11
master pages, 2, 11-12, 14, 36, 40, 64, 67, 71, 74, 113, 125
mastheads, designing, 59
mathematical copy, 78
MathType, 78
mechanicals
    creating, 26
menus, designing, 25
metallic ink, 16, 29
mezzotint effect, 126
Multiple Paste, 17, 89, 117

N

nameplates, designing, 39, 54-57, 56, 58, 59, 60
newsletters, designing, 58, 59, 60, 61, 62, 64-65
numbers, as design elements, 9

O

order forms, designing, 33
outdents, 20, 113
ovals, drawing, 43
overprinting, 97, 101, 119-124

P

page numbering, automatic, 36
pages
    inserting, 67
    moving around in a document, 3
Paper color, 19
paper, recycled, 29
paragraph spacing, 8
paragraph styles
    defining, 32, 42, 68
    defining from existing paragraph, 68
    using a "based on" style, 68
paragraph, changing type specs within, 21
paste
    multiple, 89
    power, 100
pattern, creating, 89
photographs
    brightness, adjusting, 97, 105
    coloring, 115
    contrast, adjusting, 105
    as design elements, 40
    framing, 94, 95
    grayscale

converting to bitmap, 96, 105
    scanned, 102-103
    keying for the printer, 26
    layering, 96-97, 98
    montage, 76
    negative, 97, 104
    placeholders for, 38, 72
    solarizing, 104, 105
    transparent (*see* TIFFs)
placeholders, low-resolution, 38, 72
postcards, designing, 30-31
posterization, 104-105
power paste, 100
press releases, designing sheets for, 25
printing, 7
problems, identifying, 38
production, book, 125-127
PS GroupIt, 60, 78
pull quotes, 12,16

Q

quotation marks, typographer's, 5
quotes, credit lines for, 30
quotes, pull, 12

R

reflection, 60, 92, 110-112
rotation, 95, 110-112
    constraining, 57
Rule Above, 83
Rule Below, 81, 83
rules
    with type, 51, 55, 59, 81
    vertical, as design elements, 62, 74, 75
Run Script Addition, 77
running foot, 36

S

scans as placeholders, 34, 40, 42
Scrapbook, to turn type into graphic, 47
screen display of graphics, 6
screen refresh, speeding up, 3
screens, custom halftone, 102-103, 105
separation, color, 7
series of publications, designing, 34
Set Width, 25, 29, 37, 71, 72, 74, 78
shapes, drawn, combined with type, 57
sidebars, designing, 42
signature, canned, 16

skewing, 112
small caps, 25, 80
small documents, ganging, 116-117
solarizing, 104, 105
Sort Pages Addition, 3
Space After a paragraph, 8, 20, 67
Space Before, 8
Spacing Attributes, 38
spot color, 19
spreads, rearranging, 127
stationery, designing, 24-25, 27-29
step-and-repeat, 89, 117
Story Editor, 3
Styles palette, 42
styles, paragraph, creating, 32
subheads, 36, 59, 113
subscripts, 78, 79
subtitles, designing, 43
superscripts, 56, 78, 79, 80

T

table of contents, designing 8, 9, 10, 40, 71
tables, typesetting, 82-83, 107, 114
tabs, 33, 82
technical material, designing for text blocks, resizing, 14
templates, 3, 36
text flow
    automatic, 14, 125
    semi-automatic, 14
text wrap, 16, 33, 48, 51, 96, 99
    adjusting, 37-38
    around type elements, 47
    boundary
        adding points to, 52
        deleting points from, 53
    inside a circle, 52
text
    type size and leading for, 68
texture, background, 48, 63, 81, 99
thumbnails, printing, 126
TIFFs,
    1-bit (transparent), 18, 19, 97, 98, 112
    color separation of, 7
    coloring, 18, 115
    LZW compression, 23
Tile view, 2
tints, 90

titles
    designing, 43, 54-57, 58, 59, 60, 62, 63, 64-65, 80
    emphasizing a single word of, 54
tools, operating from the keyboard, 3
track, 5, 19, 20, 29, 30, 56, 64, 71, 73, 74, 80
    maintaining, in files from earlier versions, 5
trapping, 118-124
type
    contrasting
        colors, 55
        styles, 55, 75
        weights, 54, 59
    with drawn shapes, 57
    fitting, 62
    forced justification, 31, 56, 71, 74, 75
    importing, 39, 43, 46
    mood, setting with, 74
    as ornament, 91
    outline, 55
    overlapping letters, 61
    reverse, 31, 35, 40, 41, 48, 55, 60, 63, 64, 65
    rotating, 111
    on a curve, 8
    rotating, 92
    script faces, 54, 55, 56
    shadowed, 55
    slug, defined, 65
    varying width of, 25, 37
    wrapping (*see* text wrap)
type specimen book, 66-69
type styles, 92

U

underline, 80

V

versions of a layout, tracking by date, 125
viewing imported graphics, options for, 36
views
    magnified, 3
    several files at once, 2

W

white space
    designing with 8, 20, 72, 75

Z

zooming, 3

About the Authors

Linnea Dayton is consulting editor for *Step-By-Step Electronic Design*, a full-color monthly newsletter for graphic designers and illustrators using the computer, and electronic design editor of *Step-By-Step Graphics* magazine. Formerly managing editor of *Verbum* magazine, she is coauthor of the Verbum Book series (*PostScript Illustration*, *Electronic Page Design*, *Digital Painting*, *Scanned Imagery,* and *Digital Typography*) as well as *Making Art on the Macintosh II*, *The Desktop Color Book*, *The Photo CD Book* and *The Photoshop Wow! Book*. Dayton has also written an interactive column for *Verbum Interactive,* a magazine on CD-ROM, and is interested in exploring the medium of interactive fiction. Among other accomplishments she remembers with fondness and pride are starting a thriving alternative class in the public school system, backpacking more than 150 miles in the mountains of Nepal, and fledging two offspring. She lives in Solana Beach, California.

Janet Ashford is a writer and artist focussing on computer illustration and design. She is a regular contributor to *MacUser*, *Print* and *Step-By-Step Graphics* magazines and is a contributing editor of *Step-By-Step Electronic Design* newsletter. She is coauthor of the *Verbum Book of PostScript Illustration* and contributed illustrations to the *Verbum Book of Digital Painting* and *The Desktop Color Book*. Her background in traditional fine art media and music combined with her extensive experience as a computer illustrator and designer gives her a unique understanding of the computer graphics and multimedia fields. Ashford is also the author of *The Whole Birth Catalog, Birth Stories: The Experience Remembered, Mothers & Midwives: A History of Traditional Childbirth*, and for nine years edited and published *Childbirth Alternatives Quarterly*. Her three children were born at home. When not in front of a computer, Ashford plays jigs, reels and slow airs on the fiddle with a traditional string band, Lime in the Harp. She lives in Solana Beach, California.